Native Plants of Southern Nevada

T0308864

Native Plants
of Southern Nevada

An Ethnobotany

David Rhode

THE UNIVERSITY OF UTAH PRESS

Salt Lake City

© 2002 by The University of Utah Press
All rights reserved

LIBRARY OF CONGRESS CATALOGING-IN-PUBLICATION DATA

Rhode, David, 1956–
    Native plants of southern Nevada : an ethnobotany / David Rhode.
        p. cm.
Includes bibliographical references.
    ISBN 0-87480-722-0 (pbk. : alk. paper)
    1. Indians of North America—Ethnobotany—Nevada—Handbooks,
manuals, etc. 2. Ethnobotany—Nevada—Nevada—Handbooks, manuals, etc.
3. Endemic plants—Nevada—Handbooks, manuals, etc. I. Title
    E78.N4 R46 2002
    581.6'09793—dc21
2001008032

For Allise, for all

Contents

7. Grasses and Grasslike Plants

8. Bulb Plants

Preface

This compilation of the Native uses of plants found in the southern Great Basin and northern Mojave Desert began as part of the U.S. Department of Energy's Yucca Mountain Site Characterization Project (YMP). The YMP is charged by Congress to determine if Yucca Mountain might be a suitable location for the nation's first long-term high-level nuclear waste storage repository. Why, one might ask, is the YMP interested in ethnobotany?

As part of its legal responsibilities under a mandate from Congress, the YMP has engaged in detailed environmental, historical, and cultural research of the region. The YMP has long recognized that Paiute and Shoshone peoples have strong traditional ties to Yucca Mountain. Studies were conducted in the late 1980s to document these ties and identify concerns of the Paiute and Shoshone groups that called Yucca Mountain their home. Following these initial studies, the YMP developed a program of ongoing, regular meetings with seventeen tribes and other concerned Native American organizations to discuss a wide array of project activities, issues, and concerns.

A major concern expressed by these groups has been the protection of those plants having traditional uses at Yucca Mountain. Richard Stoffle and his colleagues conducted ethnobotanical studies in the late 1980s [71, 72]. They documented the wide variety of plants found at Yucca Mountain and in the surrounding areas that were used by Native peoples living in the region in historic and prehistoric times. These studies also demonstrated a strong and abiding interest on the part of concerned Native groups toward the care, wise use, and stewardship of these plants.

These reports were limited in distribution, however, and the illustrations could not be readily used to identify plants in the wild. The consulting tribes recognized that their traditional plant lore was in danger of being lost, a loss that could be avoided if the information was available in a more accessible format. The tribes recommended that one way to protect the traditional values of plants growing at Yucca Mountain was to provide a well-illustrated, more complete guide to traditional uses and to make this guide available to tribal members, schools, and other interested people.

This compilation of Native plant uses in the land around Yucca Mountain would not be possible without the generosity of the Paiute and Shoshone people who have shared their traditional knowledge about the plants of their homeland with anthropologists and biologists. Among the consultants who provided information about the uses of plants are the following individuals: Irene Benn (Southern Paiute, Moapa), Richard Birchum (Shoshone, Austin), Mary Lou Brown (Chemehuevi, Parker), Leslie Button (Owens Valley Paiute, Lone Pine), Lila Carter (Southern Paiute, Las Vegas), Bobbi Chavez (Owens Valley Paiute, Bishop), Bill and Maude China (Southern Paiute, Moapa), Dave (Southern Paiute, Moapa), Leslie Davis (Owens Valley Paiute, Big Pine), Lana Decker (Owens Valley Paiute, Bishop), Bill Dock (Timbisha Shoshone, Death Valley), Pauline Esteves (Timbisha Shoshone, Death Valley), Dolores Gillette (Timbisha Shoshone, Death Valley), Grace Goad (Timbisha Shoshone, Death Valley), Boyd Graham (Western Shoshone, Duckwater), George Hanson (Timbisha Shoshone, Death Valley), Levi Hooper (Western Shoshone, Yomba), Andrew and Mary Howell (Southern Paiute, Ash Meadows), George Laird (Chemehuevi), Belinda Lopez (Southern Paiute, Las Vegas), Cynthia Lynch (Southern Paiute, Pahrump), Mata'vium (Southern Paiute, Las Vegas), Herbert Meyers (Southern Paiute, Moapa), Lalovi Miller (Southern Paiute, Moapa), Vernon Miller (Owens Valley Paiute, Fort Independence), Nedeen Naylor (Owens Valley Paiute, Lone Pine), Hank Patterson (Timbisha Shoshone, Death Valley), Woodrow Pete (Southern Paiute, Cedar City), Katherine Siva Saubel (Cahuilla, Palm Springs), John Shakespeare (Western Shoshone, Lida), Ike Shaw (Western Shoshone, Beatty), Maggie Shaw (Western Shoshone, Lida), Ted Shaw (Western Shoshone, Duckwater), Charles Smith (Chemehuevi, Parker), Daisy Smith (Southern Paiute, Parker), Effie Smith (Southern Paiute, Las Vegas), Mart Snow (Southern Paiute, Shivwits), Tom Stewart (Western Shoshone, Beatty), Tom Stone (Owens Valley Paiute, Fish Springs), Tony Tillohash (Southern Paiute, Kaibab), Louella Tom (Southern Paiute, Moapa), Leila Wilder (Owens Valley Paiute, Fort Independence), Emma Williams (Kawaiisu, Paiute Rancheria), and Marie Wilson (Southern Paiute, Las Vegas). Other individuals have contributed to the legacy of knowledge passed down to the present, but their names are not known and so cannot be included here.

I also extend my appreciation to the anthropologists, botanists, and other interested persons who sought out and wrote down this information for posterity. Individuals included in this long effort include W. Andrew Archer, David P. Barrows, Lowell John Bean, Frederick W. Coville, Frederick Dellenbaugh, Michael Evans, Catherine S. Fowler, David Halmo, John P. Harrington, Mark R. Harrington, James Henrichs, Isabel T. Kelly, Mark Kerr, Alfred Kroeber, Carobeth Laird, Edith Van Allen Murphey, Wesley Niles, Joan O'Farrell, Edward Palmer, John Wesley Powell, Edward Sapir, Julian H. Steward, Kenneth M. Stewart, Omer C. Stewart, Richard Stoffle, Percy Train, Richard Van Valkenburgh, William J. Wallace, and Maurice Zigmond.

Finally, this volume would not exist in its present form without the continued support and contributions of several institutions and individuals. Wendy Dixon, Scott Wade, and William Freeland (YMP) strongly supported this project from its inception. Greg Fasano, Vicki Best, and Richard Arnold (Science Applications International Corporation [SAIC]) spent many hours coordinating with concerned Native American individuals and the Consolidated Group of Tribes and Organizations (CGTO), an informal confederation representing seventeen separate Southern Paiute, Western Shoshone, and Owens Valley Paiute tribes and organizations. The CGTO has consulted with the YMP for nearly ten years, and their endorsements and recommendations regarding this project were a major reason for its existence. Several members of the CGTO reviewed a draft of this ethnobotany and generously provided useful comments and new information. These reviewers included Richard Arnold (Pahrump Paiute Tribe), Jerry Charles (Ely Shoshone), Pauline Esteves (Timbisha Shoshone), Yetta Jake (Paiute Indian Tribe of Utah), Cynthia Lynch (Pahrump Paiute Tribe), Vernon Miller (Fort Independence Paiute Tribe of Owens Valley), and Bertha Moose (Big Pine Paiute Tribe of Owens Valley). Greg Fasano, Vicki Best, Kevin Blomquist (SAIC), Tom O'Farrell (SAIC), and Don Powers (SAIC) also reviewed various drafts. Dr. Catherine S. Fowler (University of Nevada, Reno) provided inspiration, valuable comments on a previous draft, and access to unpublished field notes of Dr. Isabel Kelly. Saxon Sharpe (Desert Research Institute [DRI]) assisted in research and descriptions of several of the plants, and Annette Risley (DRI) assisted with the graphics. Jeff Grathwohl (University of Utah Press) and Lisa DiDonato provided valuable editorial assistance. The Anna Lander West McDowell Endowment provided partial support for publication costs. Photographs and permission to use them were provided by the National Park Service (Death Valley National Park), U.S. Borax and Chemical Corporation, Mr. Gary Steward, the University of Illinois Archives, and the Nevada Historical Society. I extend my thanks to all.

Introduction

In 1891 a young botanist named Frederick Coville spent several months exploring Death Valley and the surrounding desert areas in southern Nevada and southeastern California, a region barely known to biological science at the time. Twenty-four years old and fresh out of college in upstate New York, Coville had just gotten a job with the U.S. Department of Agriculture. He had not traveled west before. To his eastern eyes, the deserts held striking beauty but also stark desolation. Coville wrote [12]:

> To a traveler passing by rail across our southwestern desert region it is a matter of great wonder how the Indians of that country contrive to subsist. Those who are not familiar with the desert can imagine an apparently unlimited plain, devoid of trees and grass, without streams or springs, but provided with a vegetation of cactus and scattered low shrubs of greasewood and creosote bush. Nor does a closer inspection affect one more pleasantly, for all the shrubbery is either woody and indigestible, or resinous and rank both in smell and taste. There appear to be no animals but lizards, an occasional rattlesnake, and sometimes an abundance of hungry-looking jack-rabbits. The very first necessaries of life appear to be absolutely wanting, and this state of affairs exists not for one mile only, nor for ten miles, but for hundreds.

Yet hundreds of generations of Native peoples had found ways to survive in this arid land through thousands of seasons, making use of dozens of different kinds of plants and animals for food, tools, clothing, shelter, and medicine. For these people, the deserts and mountains of their homeland are not stark and forbidding, but rather a place of secret plenty, if one only knows where to look. Coville learned this lesson, too, and went on to write a classic description of the rich plant life of the Mojave Desert and a pioneering report on the ethnobotany of some of its Native inhabitants [12, 13].

Where, then, does one look? This book examines some of the most important plants used by the Paiute and Shoshone people of southern Nevada. It draws on nineteenth-century accounts of exploring botanists and anthropologists such as Coville and more detailed ethnobotanical research conducted by numerous anthropologists, in collaboration with Native experts, since the 1930s. We begin our examination of southern Nevada's ethnobotany by first setting the context and the main players: the region, its major plant communities, and the Native peoples who call it home.

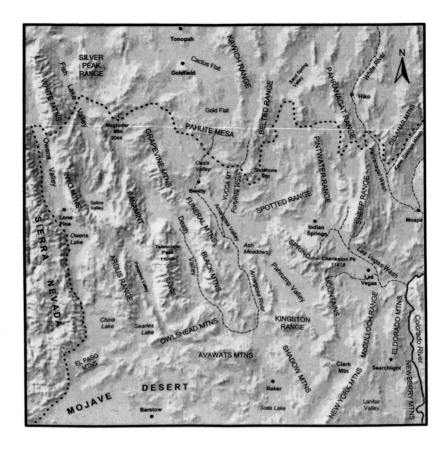

Figure 1. Southern Nevada's deserts: the northern Mojave Desert–southern Great Basin region. The black dotted line marks the approximate edge of typical Mojave Desert vegetation, bordering the Sierra Nevada on the west and the Great Basin floristic province to the north.

The Region and Its Plant Associations

Our area of interest centers on two deserts that merge together in southern Nevada, the Mojave and Great Basin (Figure 1). The Mojave Desert is a warm desert, having fairly low valley elevations (from below sea level in Death Valley to about 3000 feet), cool winters, and scorching summers. In contrast, the Great Basin Desert is characterized as a cold desert, with significantly higher valley elevations (4500–6000 feet), usually cold winters, and summers that are warm but much milder than the brutal thermal belt to the south. These physiographic and climatic differences result in two very different floristic provinces—the transition found in southwestern Nevada.

Within these distinctive floristic regions are equally dramatic elevation gradients produced by intervening valleys and mountains: from low-

Figure 2. A view from the top of Yucca Mountain, looking southeast toward Mount Charleston

elevation oases and playas; outward into the dry desert flats, bajadas, and smaller desert mountain ranges; and upward to the woodlands, forests, meadows, and alpine barrens of the higher mountains (Figure 2). This topographic mosaic supports a variety of plant communities, assorted according to physiography, soil, climate, latitude, and elevation [5].

Valley Oases

Some valleys contain permanent springs or groundwater shallow enough to be accessible to plants. Ash Meadows is a good example of such an oasis (Figure 3). The numerous springs that bubble up here sustain an abundant plant community. Trees such as velvet ash (*Fraxinus velutina*), screwbean mesquite (*Prosopis pubescens*), western honey mesquite (*Prosopis glandulosa*), willow (*Salix exigua* and *Salix gooddingii*), and Fremont's cottonwood (*Populus fremontii*) form thickets and open woodlands, accompanied by a variety of moisture-loving shrubs, vines, grassy meadows, and marsh or aquatic plants. Most of these water lovers are not found in the arid surrounding countryside. The meadows, wetlands, and woodlands form a mosaic with surrounding shrublands, which are dominated by plants that can tolerate the characteristic fine-grained, alkaline, and occasionally saturated soils [5]. Such plants include inland saltgrass (*Distichlis spicata*), shadscale (*Atriplex confertifolia*), and Mojave seablite (*Suaeda moquinii*). Surrounding these wetlands and playas near the valley bottoms, plant communities dominated by shadscale, desert holly (*Atriplex hymenelytra*), fourwing saltbush (*Atriplex*

Figure 3. Alkaline meadow and marsh plant communities at Ash Meadows

canescens), and Torrey jointfir (*Ephedra torreyana*) are common (Figure 4). Low-growing thickets of mesquite often grow on sand dunes in these communities.

Mojave Desert Shrub Associations

Further upslope from these valley-bottom communities, on the dry and gravelly alluvial slopes or bajadas, grow plant communities dominated by shrubs typical of vast areas of the Mojave Desert. These plants are inured to persistent drought, hot summers, and cool winters. Chief among these is creosote bush (*Larrea tridentata*), a tall, spreading shrub of olive-green hue. This species grows at elevations below about 5200 feet, alongside a number of smaller subdominant shrubs that form a series of intergrading plant associations. Mojave Desert shrub associations do not segregate into highly distinctive, rigidly bounded communities. Instead, different species mix according to subtle habitat preferences, such as soil texture and depth, the number of days of frost, summer and winter moisture availability, and the compatibility of neighboring plants. The plant associations used herein are drawn from the work of Janice Beatley, a botanist who spent years studying the plant communities in southern Nevada [5]. Beatley recognized several plant associations and named them after the principal dominant shrubs. Recent work in the northern Mojave Desert shows that the plant ecology is more complex and gradational than Beatley's classification allows [23, 24, 39, 40], but her groupings convey much of the variability of plant habitats and the ways that topographic factors affect their distribution.

Figure 4. Mojave Desert shrubs dominated by shadscale *(Atriplex confertifolia)* and desert holly *(Atriplex hymenelytra)* on low alluvial fans around a dry lakebed (playa). Green thickets of western honey mesquite *(Prosopis glandulosa* var. *torreyana)* grow in sand dunes in the middle distance.

Where sediments are deep and sandy, creosote bush pairs up with white burrobush *(Ambrosia dumosa)* to form the *Larrea-Ambrosia* association ⌊5⌋. Creosote bush and white burrobush are the dominant shrubs, and other shrubs such as wolfberry *(Lycium andersonii* or *Lycium cooperi)*, Fremont's dalea *(Psorothamnus fremontii)*, Nevada jointfir *(Ephedra nevadensis)*, little-leaf ratany *(Krameria erecta)*, and winterfat *(Krascheninnikovia lanata)* are common associates (Figure 5). Indian ricegrass *(Achnatherum hymenoides)* is an important range grass in this community that thrives in sandy areas. On ground surfaces that have a better-developed surface pavement and where the soils are underlain by a calcareous hardpan (caliche), creosote bush co-dominates with shadscale to form the *Larrea-Atriplex* association [5]. This association is found on lower bajadas, in a complex mosaic with the *Larrea-Ambrosia* association. Fremont's dalea and littleleaf ratany are common associates, as are Mojave yucca *(Yucca schidigera)* and beavertail pricklypear *(Opuntia basilaris)*.

On the upper margins of the alluvial bajadas and in the dry desert ranges, a transition zone is reached between the warm-desert Mojave and the cold-desert Great Basin vegetation [5]. Here creosote bush and white burrobush drop out as dominant shrubs and are replaced by blackbrush *(Coleogyne ramosissima)* or by shrubs such as spiny hopsage *(Grayia spinosa)*, wolfberry, and shadscale. Blackbrush dominates on upper alluvial slopes at elevations above

Figure 5. Mojave Desert creosote bush-burrobush *(Larrea-Ambrosia)* plant association dominating alluvial valley slopes and flats

4000 feet, in the *Coleogyne* association [5]. Here, blackbrush may grow by itself in nearly pure stands or may mix with creosote bush, with other shrubs such as wolfberry, Nevada jointfir, banana yucca *(Yucca baccata)*, and eastern Mojave buckwheat *(Eriogonum fasciculatum;* Figure 6).

Elsewhere on upper bajadas and on adjacent steeper rocky slopes of lower mountains in the Mojave Desert are plant communities dominated by spiny hopsage or wolfberry, known as the *Grayia-Lycium* association [5]. These plant associations contain a variety of associated shrubs and herbs, especially Nevada jointfir or green Mormon tea *(Ephedra viridis),* eastern Mojave buckwheat, broom snakeweed *(Gutierrezia sarothrae),* desert needlegrass *(Achnatherum speciosum),* and Cooper's heathgoldenbush *(Ericameria cooperi).* They also often include the conspicuous Joshua tree *(Yucca brevifolia;* Figure 7).

Great Basin Shrublands and Woodlands

To the north and at higher elevations, the Mojave Desert plant communities disappear, being replaced by plants better adapted to survive the cold winters of the Great Basin [5]. Shrubby plant communities dominated by shadscale, fourwing saltbush, or greasewood *(Sarcobatus vermiculatus)* cover closed valleys between 4500–5500 feet elevation. Greasewood typically dominates on playa margins, often in pure stands (Figure 8) or sometimes in the company of the salt-loving seepweed *(Suaeda moquinii)* or pickleweed *(Allenrolfea occidentalis).* Surrounding these playa communities, the lower

Figure 6. Blackbrush *(Coleogyne ramosissima)* and banana yucca *(Yucca baccata)* plant association on upper alluvial fans and bajadas in the Mojave Desert. The taller plants in the background are Joshua trees *(Yucca brevifolia)*.

Figure 7. Hopsage-wolfberry *(Grayia-Lycium)* plant association, with numerous Joshua trees *(Yucca brevifolia)*, typical of upper valley slopes and low desert mountains in the Mojave Desert.

Figure 8. A nearly pure stand of greasewood *(Sarcobatus vermiculatus)* community covering a playa floor in the Great Basin

Figure 9. Shadscale saltbush *(Atriplex confertifolia)* plant association covering a valley floor in the cooler Great Basin

valley floors are dominated by shadscale, in association with winterfat and other low shrubs adapted to heavy silt soils and cold air (Figure 9). Fourwing saltbush dominates on deep, sandy soils of the type that the *Larrea-Ambrosia* association would occupy at lower elevations or more southerly latitudes.

INTRODUCTION

Figure 10. Big sagebrush *(Artemisia tridentata)* and grass plant association covering a Great Basin valley floor

At slightly higher elevations, fourwing saltbush gives way to big sagebrush *(Artemisia tridentata)* as the dominant shrub (Figure 10). Big sagebrush dominates over large areas on upper slopes of Great Basin valleys, sometimes in association with spiny hopsage, Nevada jointfir, winterfat, and rabbitbrush *(Chrysothamnus viscidiflorus, Ericameria nauseosa)* and sometimes in pure stands. On shallow rocky soils in the same area, the smaller black sagebrush *(Artemisia nova)* replaces big sagebrush.

At elevations of about 6000–8000 feet, sagebrush is accompanied by pygmy conifer trees, including Utah juniper *(Juniperus osteosperma)* and singleleaf pinyon pine *(Pinus monophylla),* to form an open woodland (Figure 11). This steppe-woodland mosaic covers the slopes and ridges of mountain ranges in much of the Great Basin, including the middle elevations of the Spring Range in southern Nevada [5]. In southern Nevada, this community also sometimes contains stands of Gambel's oak *(Quercus gambelii)* and a wide variety of montane shrubs and herbs. Sagebrush steppe without woodland communities may intersperse with the woodlands, and many higher mountains have an upper sagebrush zone located above the limits of pinyon and juniper (Figure 12).

Montane Forests and Meadows

On higher mountains such as Mount Charleston (Figure 13), other conifers appear, such as white fir (*Abies concolor*), ponderosa pine (*Pinus ponderosa*), or limber pine (*Pinus flexilis*). At these high elevations,

Figure 11. Pinyon-juniper *(Pinus-Juniperus)* woodlands in the Spring Range

Figure 12. Upper sagebrush *(Artemisia tridentata)* zone covering mountain slopes above pinyon-juniper woodlands

temperatures are cool enough and rainfall sufficiently high to support water-loving plants such as quaking aspen (*Populus tremuloides*), willow (*Salix* spp.) Woods' rose (*Rosa woodsii*), elderberry (*Sambucus cerulea*), and currant (*Ribes* spp.). Slopes not covered with conifers are often clothed with

Figure 13. Conifer forest and alpine shrub communities on Mount Charleston

curlleaf mountain mahogany (*Cercocarpus ledifolius*), Stansbury cliffrose (*Purshia stansburiana*), Utah serviceberry (*Amelanchier utahensis*), and sagebrush. On the very highest mountains of the region, subalpine trees such as limber pine and Great Basin bristlecone pine (*Pinus longaeva*) form a sparse woodland in association with low alpine meadows and barrens.

The People

The southern Great Basin and northern Mojave Desert region is home to several different Paiute and Shoshone peoples, all of whom speak Numic languages (Figure 14): the Owens Valley Paiute, who live in Owens Valley, between the White Mountains and the Sierra Nevada; the Western Shoshone, who inhabit much of the Great Basin; the closely related Timbisha Shoshone (or Panamint), who live in Death Valley and environs; and the Southern Paiute (including the Chemehuevi), whose homeland is the eastern Mojave Desert from eastern California to Utah. According to many anthropologists, the ancient homeland common to all of these people lies within the area covered by this ethnobotany [30].

Paiute and Shoshone social life was organized mainly around the family group or family cluster as the basic social and economic unit. Larger social groupings would coalesce when the resource base provided the opportunity, such as during rabbit drives or mesquite harvests, or for certain ceremonies [48, 66]. Social relationships tended to be largely egalitarian, although certain people attained measures of status through prowess, experience, or

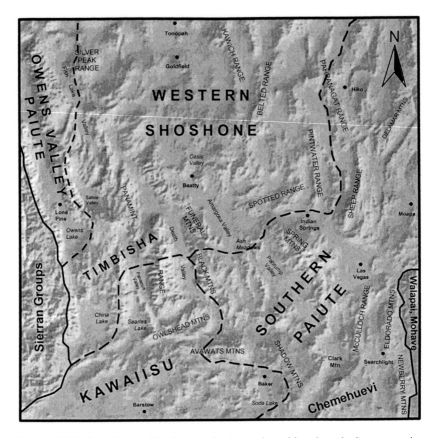

Figure 14. The homelands of Native peoples in southern Nevada and adjacent southeastern California

special knowledge (both practical and esoteric). Better-watered areas, such as Owens Valley, supported more stable communities and larger populations, and it appears that social hierarchy and property ownership was slightly more developed there. However, these well-populated oases were the exception in this mostly arid region.

These Paiute and Shoshone societies shared a way of life based mainly on harvesting wild plants and animals. Food resources varied greatly in abundance depending on the season, the location, and the year. In a given locality, wild nut and seed crops might abound one year and fail miserably for the next two or three. Usually, no one locality contained sufficient foodstuffs throughout the year to support a group, so making a living by hunting and gathering in this region meant that people moved many times during the annual cycle to gather resources from different localities.

Generally, Paiute and Shoshone people spent spring and early summer in the valleys, subsisting on greens, bulbs, agave hearts, and early seed crops. As summer wore on and valley plants dried up in the desert heat, many people followed the green to cooler and moister upper elevations, whereas others stayed close to scattered springside oases in the valleys. Those individuals who had stayed in the lower valleys, such as Death Valley, collected ripe pods of mesquite and screwbean. In late summer, pine nuts were ready for harvest in the mountains. Winters were generally spent in valley villages, but families might spend winters in the mountains if pine nut crops were exceptionally good. In some areas, certain families owned favorite mesquite or pinyon groves, returning to camp year after year and defending them from other would-be harvesters. Other families could often collect in these areas, however, if permission was first obtained.

The generations of experience gained in this annual cycle and the reliance placed on native plants for all the necessaries of life, made the Paiute and Shoshone people knowledgeable botanists and plant managers. People knew well their homeland's plants and habitats. They kept close watch for the often very short span of time that seed crops were available—missing an important seed crop could mean great hunger or worse. People learned the intricacies of which crops ripened when in various localities scattered over a vast landscape. They learned which plants and plant parts were useful for curing certain ailments, which produced colorful dyes, which could keep spirits away, which could poison an arrow tip. Most individuals learned the ways and uses of various plants both from their elders and in the course of their daily lives, as they needed to. In a region where a small family group was often on its own for days or weeks at a time, knowledge of the region's plants and their uses was crucial for self-sufficiency and survival. Although some individuals might have special knowledge, skill, or affinity with certain plants and plant products, in general most people carried with them a good working knowledge of the region's plants.

The people also knew the conditions under which various plants provided the greatest yields, and they worked to improve the production of native stands in many ways [31, 33]. That many of the harvested plants are thought to be "wild" does not mean they were unmanaged—indeed, the dubious line between wild and cultivated is nowhere more blurred than here. Shrubby areas were sometimes burned to improve the growth of seed plants. Mesquite groves were cleaned and pruned to enhance the seed harvest, and other trees were pruned or beaten to increase yields. Plots of important plants, such as willow or tobacco, were set aside and closely tended. In the better-watered Owens Valley, groups augmented the wild harvest by cultivating and irrigating a few native root and seed crops [65]. Elsewhere in the Great Basin, people sowed wild seeds in favorable localities to increase the next year's yield or transplanted certain plants to increase their range [66]. Small-scale gardening of introduced maize and squash was practiced in some localities by the early nineteenth century, and possibly a few hundred years earlier [31, 32, 85]. But such gardening was always limited in scale, only supplementing the traditional resources available throughout this region.

Several other Native groups occupied lands adjacent to this region. The Kawaiisu, who spoke a language related to Southern Paiute, lived in the Tehachapi Mountains and southern Sierra Nevada and the western Mojave Desert, just west of our area. Anthropologist Maurice Zigmond [87] explored in detail the Kawaiisu knowledge and uses of plants. The Serrano and Cahuilla people, speakers of languages in the Takic family, traditionally lived along the Mojave River and in the mountains bordering the Mojave Desert to the south and southwest of our area; excellent ethnobotanies for the Cahuilla are available [2, 3, 4]. Along the Colorado River live the Yuman-speaking Mojave and Walapai peoples, who typically relied more heavily on the cultivation of maize, beans, and squash than did the Paiute and Shoshone discussed here. Uses of plants by these groups are described in several sources [e.g., 6, 10, 68, 69].

Useful Plants

This book illustrates nearly one hundred species from more than forty plant families that are recognized as useful in various ways by the Native people who live in the southern Great Basin and northern Mojave Desert. This book is not meant to be a comprehensive ethnobotany of the region or of any single group (e.g., Zigmond's ethnobotany of the Kawaiisu people [87] lists nearly 340 different plants). Nor is it a technical botanical treatise or plant identification key, although the general character of each plant is described. Instead, the book describes some of the most important and useful native plants in the area, together with Native terms for the plants and a description of the ways in which the plants were used.

These plants are found in a variety of different habitats in southern Nevada, ranging from dry valley bottoms to moist mountain canyons. Some of these plants are common or dominant members of their plant communities, whereas others are quite rare. The plants have a multitude of uses. About 70 percent of the species were used for food, 60 percent for medicine or hygiene, 20 percent as a source of fibers or raw materials for textiles and basketry, 35 percent for the manufacture of other utilitarian articles, 20 percent for construction of dwellings or other structures, 15 percent for fuel, 10 percent for ceremonial or ritual purposes, and about 20 percent for other purposes such as games, chewing gum, adornment, or bouquets.

Paiute and Shoshone people consider the various uses of these plants to be an important factor in their plant classification schemes [29]. For example, the Chemehuevi group of Southern Paiute divides all plants and animals into two basic groups: what is eaten and what is not eaten (including medicine). Each category is then further divided into plants and animals, and the plants in each group are further subdivided into land and water plants. The land plants are separated into various categories based on the use to which the plant is put (seed crop, root crop, leaf crop, cultivated plants, medicines, plants that are no good) or on life form (tree, shrub, vine, thorny plant, herb, flower, grass). The Western Shoshone share essentially the same classification scheme, adjusting for certain differences in the plants that are characteristic of present-day Southern Paiute and Shoshone homelands.

In some cases, names of plants or plant parts reflect multiple uses. For example, skunkbush sumac *(Rhus trilobata)* has small red berries that are used for food, and the Southern Paiute classify the berries under the what-is-eaten category. The stems of the same plant are used for basketry, and these are classified under the what-is-not-eaten category. Names of specific plants may also reflect their habitat, color, smell, or other distinguishing features.

Format of the Book

The concept of plant usage is very important in Native classifications, and describing Native uses of plants is the purpose of this book. Organizing the plants by usage is not practicable, however, because many plants have multiple uses. For instance, what grouping would sagebrush fit in—food, medicine, textiles, or construction? The answer is all of them. To avoid redundancy, another scheme is required.

The scheme adopted here is based primarily on life form: trees, large woody shrubs and vines, smaller subshrubs, yuccas and agaves, cacti, annual and perennial broadleaf herbs, grasses and grasslike plants, and bulb plants. Within these categories of life form, plants generally appear in this book according to where they usually grow along a transect of rising elevation: from valley-bottom oases through dry desert flats and smaller mountains, then to the higher forested reaches of the larger ranges in the region.

For each plant, a description of its morphology and habitat is given, followed by its uses. Common and scientific names used throughout the book follow recent regional floras [1, 14–18, 41, 82]. Scientific names of plants sometimes change as more becomes known about relationships between different plant species and populations, and other authorities may have used a different, older name (or synonym) for the same plant species. The U.S. Department of Agriculture's National Plants Database website (http://plants. usda.gov) maintains current common and scientific names as well as a synonymy of older epithets, which is very helpful for perusing the older ethnobotanical literature.

The information gathered here includes the work of numerous anthropologists, botanists, linguists, and other scholars. Their works are cited in the text by numbers enclosed in brackets, and each number corresponds to the full bibliographic entry at the end of the book. A *Sources* section at the end of each plant description lists the author and date of each reference. This system is used in the hopes that the reader can more easily follow the text without the constant interruption of author-date citations, but if so inclined can still track down the original reference.

A plethora of Native names are listed for some plants. The Native terms for plants differ between languages or dialects, even though all the Native groups included in this ethnobotany spoke related Numic languages. Different names may reflect different plant parts or different plant uses. They may also simply reflect the way explorers, botanists, and anthropologists heard and transcribed what their Native consultants told them. Some of these recorders had training in linguistic methods and orthography, whereas others did not. Rather than translate all terms into a standard orthography, the choice has been made to keep the spelling of the Native terms as they were originally recorded. Those based on common English sounds are placed in quotation marks, whereas those written in phonetic notation are without quotes. Different authors use symbols in slightly different ways to represent sounds, however, and the reader should consult the individual reference to determine which symbols go with which sounds in specific instances.

A Word of Caution

The plants in this book have all been described in the literature as being useful to Native people in southern Nevada. This does not mean, however, that they can or should be used without due caution. Many plants (or certain parts of plants) contain chemicals that can be very dangerous if ingested in the wrong doses or in combination with other substances. Other plants are thorny, spiny, poisonous, or may otherwise cause physical discomfort if picked. Native American people believe that certain prescriptions must be followed for a plant to work properly. For example, certain plants must be collected from particular areas or at specific times. A system of traditional beliefs and methods attend the collection and use of plants, traditions that involve elements of respect, approach, preparation, dosage, administration, and/or consumption of foods or medicines. The reader should not consume any plant parts without proper knowledge, training, and oversight, because allergic reactions or severe illness could result. Neither the author nor the publisher endorses the use of the plants described herein as food or medicine, nor do they assume any liability for the actions of the reader.

Native American people believe that plants are found in certain areas for a reason and that they are tied to traditional stories or beliefs. Many plant species are rare and should be protected, not picked. Care should be exercised to avoid damaging plants in certain areas, even though they may appear to be abundant. Federal and state law may protect plants from damage or unauthorized collection.

CHAPTER ONE

Trees

Pea Family (Fabaceae)

Western Honey Mesquite

Prosopis glandulosa Torr. var. *torreyana* (L. Benson) M. C. Johnston

Figures 15–19

Owens Valley Paiute: *"ah-pee"* [55]
Southern Paiute: *o'pimb* [71]; *'opimpɨ* [50]; *kakɨmpi* (seeds only) [50];
 obi (pods) [32]; *"be-avah"* [49]; *opⁱ* [70]; *hopiʰimp'* [66];
 hopimp [75]; *hopihimpⁱ* [66]
Timbisha Shoshone: *"oveehimbi"* [25]; *ohbi* (pods) [32];
 "o-vee" (mature pods) [25, 49]; *"o-ho-bi," "o-have"* (flowers) [49];
 "ovee-ha-ve-gin" (blooms) [25]; *"sea-vee"* (young green pod) [25, 49];
 "mombeasea" (leaves) [49]; *"bea-shee"* (leaves) [25]
Western Shoshone: *o'phi* [71]

Description and Habitat

Western honey mesquite is a many-branched thorny tree or large shrub that grows to 10–25 feet tall [1, 41]. The leaves are long and narrow, composed of small linear leaflets that grow opposite one another on a long central stalk, or pinna [7]. Small yellow flowers are borne in narrow pendulous tassels that are about 2 inches long [1]. After flowering, the tree bears a wealth of thin flat green pods, which later fill out with beans and turn brown and dry.

Western honey mesquite typically grows in sandy valleys below 3000 feet elevation, although small nonreproducing plants are known to grow at elevations up to 4800 feet [5]. This tree is deeply rooted and able to tap fairly deep groundwater sources, so western honey mesquite is not completely restricted to well-watered valley oases, as are other trees such as screwbean mesquite *(Prosopis pubescens)*. Dunes often coalesce around shrubby forms of mesquite, burying much of the plant [7, 41].

Native Uses

Mesquite was an important food wherever it was available in the Mojave Desert [3, 4, 9, 32], and indeed throughout the arid Southwest [6, 27, 28]. People often camped in mesquite groves in Death Valley and Ash Meadows,

Figure 15. Western honey mesquite *(Prosopis glandulosa* var. *torreyana)*

Figure 16. Honey mesquite *(Prosopis glandulosa* var. *torreyana)* foliage and flower clusters

where the trees provided shade, adequate firewood, and abundant edible pods and the groves attracted game animals. In Ash Meadows, families owned particular mesquite groves and routinely cleared them of under-growth to make it easier to live among the thorny trees and gather the

Figure 17. Unripe green pods of western honey mesquite *(Prosopis glandulosa* var. *torreyana)*

pods [66]. Trees were pruned to establish camping areas, provide firewood, and help new seedlings develop [33].

In late spring, when young green pods made their appearance, Timbisha people pit-roasted the pods over hot stones to make a tart food [32]. The Timbisha made a tea from the leaves, and both leaves and flowers were boiled as greens [49]. Timbisha mothers sometimes chewed mesquite leaves and applied the dressing to ant bites on their children [25]. Southern Paiute people ate the green pods raw as snacks, seeking out trees with the sweetest pods [32]. Shoshone people near Owens Valley boiled the young pods like string beans [67]. In historic times the Shoshone made a soup with mesquite pods, bacon, onion, tomatoes, and potatoes [56].

When the pods had ripened but not yet dried, they were pounded and mashed to make a sweet juice drink. This refreshing drink sometimes contained gum from the mesquite bark as well [56]. The Chemehuevi parched the ripened beans in a basket with hot coals [50].

Once the pods were mature and dried, Southern Paiute families gathered them up in earnest, and the women pounded them in large wooden mortars

Figure 18. Ripened dry pods of honey mesquite *(Prosopis glandulosa* var. *torreyana)* and screwbean *(Prosopis pubescens)*

to make a nutritious meal [32]. The meal was made into a mush that was the base for all stews or it was formed into a large cake. To make a mesquite cake, the meal was packed into a large conical burden basket, set out in the sun to dry, and left to harden for a few days. In rainy weather, the basket would be placed near the fire inside a person's shelter. After this process of drying and slow-cooking, the basket was inverted and removed, revealing a dense, cone-shaped lump of meal weighing 50–60 pounds [75]. Pieces of the meal-cake were broken off to make soups and stews or were eaten directly. A few pieces of meal-cake were good trail food: one man said, "'Hopimp good! Eat two little pieces and you can run after deer all day" [75]. These cakes were stored for later use. Sometimes the large cakes were kept underground in specially prepared pits lined with grass, which were dug into the dirt floors of rock shelters [67, 75].

The Timbisha often collected the ripe pods in autumn, cached them until spring, then pounded them to make flour for loaves [13, 67]. The hard seeds, which did not grind up with the pods, were sifted out and later ground on a metate for food [32] or were thrown away [67]. The Timbisha also stored seeds in caves for later use [67]. One such cache of western honey mesquite seeds was recently found in Breakfast Canyon, in Death Valley [85].

Elsewhere in the Mojave Desert [4, 10], Mohave and Cahuilla people stored mesquite pods in large specially built granaries woven from branches of willow (*Salix* spp.) or arrowweed (*Pluchea sericea*), set atop stilts. Each granary, which looked like a giant bird's nest, could store from ten to forty

Figure 19. Annie Shoshone (Timbisha) grinds dried mesquite pods on a metate. This photograph was probably staged and is not accurate. Typically, women pounded mesquite pods in wooden mortars using stone pestles and did not grind them directly on flat metates, as shown here. (Photograph by H. F. Cameron, courtesy of the National Park Service, Death Valley National Park)

bushels (up to 800 pounds) of dried mesquite pods. This amount, which could be harvested in a few days' time, served a family's needs for a year.

A sample of western honey mesquite flour produced from beans collected at Ash Meadows contained 5.6 percent protein, 14 percent fat, and 47.5 percent carbohydrates, for a total yield of 1536 calories per pound. It has been estimated that two women pounding away could produce about 88 pounds of flour in a day, if a helper supplied them with seeds [28]. That amount of flour would contain more than 135,000 calories, or about 5600 calories per person-hour of work (assuming each person worked an eight-hour day). That is a high rate of caloric return when compared with experimental results involving traditional gathering and processing of other plants [64]. It compares well with cattail pollen (ranked at 2750–9360 calories per person-hour) and is several times the return rate of pinyon pine nuts (840–1400 calories per person-hour). Viewed from another angle, the 88 pounds of mesquite flour made in a single day could easily supply enough food energy to support three adults for more than three weeks! It is a small wonder, then, that people throughout the arid Southwest collected western honey mesquite pods as a staple late-summer crop [3, 4, 6, 8, 10, 13, 27, 28, 31, 32, 68, 69].

Mesquite was a favorite firewood in valley camps. The coals hold high heat for a long time, making it an excellent cooking fuel. Today a mesquite stick serves as a ceremonial fire poker in the Native American Church, where the wood is considered sacred [43]. People used western honey mesquite branches to construct dwellings, and the Timbisha made wooden mortars from mesquite wood, which in turn were used to pound mesquite pods [25]. The Moapa Southern Paiute fashioned arrow tips from fire-hardened mesquite sticks, attaching them to shafts of common reed *(Phragmites australis)* with an adhesive made from creosote bush *(Larrea tridentata)* [58]. Moapa people also made bows from mesquite branches, calling such bows *"pemp"* [58].

Sources: [1] Barneby 1989; [3] Bean and Saubel 1963; [4] Bean and Saubel 1972; [5] Beatley 1976; [6] Bell and Castetter 1937; [7] Benson and Darrow 1981; [8] Buck and DuBarton 1994; [9] Bye 1972; [10] Castetter and Bell 1951; [12] Coville 1892; [13] Coville 1893; [25] P. Estevez, pers. commun.; [27] Felger 1977; [28] Felger and Moser 1985; [31] Fowler 1986; [32] Fowler 1995; [33] Fowler 1996; [41] Hickman 1993; [43] Y. Jake, pers. commun.; [49] Kerr 1936; [50] Laird 1976; [55] V. Miller, pers. commun.; [56] B. Moose, pers. commun.; [58] Murphey 1959; [64] Simms 1987; [66] Steward 1938; [67] Steward 1941; [68] Stewart 1965; [69] Stewart 1983; [70] Stewart 1942; [75] Stuart 1945; [85] Yohe 1997.

Pea Family (Fabaceae)

Screwbean Mesquite
Prosopis pubescens Benth.

Figures 18, 20, 21

Owens Valley Paiute: *"pie-eu," "or-vee"* [49]; *"pie-lu-or-ute"* [56]
Southern Paiute: *wi'ump, kweirum* [71]; *"quee-et-umb"* [78];
   kwiyarampɨ [50]; *kwiyara* (bean pod) [50]
Timbisha Shoshone: *"o-him-bah"* [49]; *"kuh-wear-room-b"* [25]

Description and Habitat

Screwbean mesquite is a thorny tree or large shrub that is closely related to western honey mesquite. It grows up to 20–30 feet high [7, 42]. Screwbean mesquite often grows in dense thickets along rich sandy or loamy bottom-lands along streams or wet areas. Screwbean mesquite leaves, like those of western honey mesquite, are composed of numerous leaflets opposed along a central stem, but the screwbean leaflets are short, oval, and hairy, unlike the long, smooth, hairless honey mesquite leaflets [1, 7]. Flower tassels are yellow and spikelike. The fruits are tightly coiled pods in bunches of two to ten that ripen during summer [7]. Screwbean is plentiful at Ash Meadows and

Figure 20. Screwbean *(Prosopis pubescens)*

Figure 21. Ripened screwbean *(Prosopis pubescens)* fruits

in other well-watered low-lying valleys to the south, where its roots can gain access to shallow groundwater sources [5].

Native Uses

Although less common than western honey mesquite in the Mojave Desert, screwbean mesquite was an important and highly favored food wherever it was found [32]. Pods were collected in summer and cured in a prepared pit lined with arrowweed *(Pluchea sericea),* where they fermented for about a month until they sweetened and turned red. Once out of the pit, the cured pods were stored or processed into meal. The small hard seeds were ground separately and mixed with water to make a refreshing and nutritious drink. Many people prized the ripened screwbean pods, which were traded widely. As one woman noted, "Many used to trade rabbitskin blanket, sheep hide, eagle feathers, sinew, anything they had, for screwbean" [32]. Some people also chewed on the young pods, without benefit of curing or processing [43].

Screwbean served palliative functions as well. A sap from the bark of the tree was soaked in water to make a medicinal eyewash [78]. Large trees gave welcome shade from oppressive summer heat [43].

Sources: [1] Barneby 1989; [5] Beatley 1976; [7] Benson and Darrow 1981; [25] P. Esteves, pers. commun.; [32] Fowler 1995; [42] Jaeger 1941; [43] Y. Jake, pers. commun.; [49] Kerr 1936; [50] Laird 1976; [56] B. Moose, pers. commun.; [71] Stoffle et al. 1989; [78] Train et al. 1941.

Olive Family (Oleaceae)

Velvet Ash
Fraxinus velutina Torr.

Singleleaf Ash
Fraxinus anomala Torr. ex S. Wats.

Figures 22–24

Southern Paiute: *"ya-peep-a"* [53]

Description and Habitat

Velvet ash is a large spreading tree that grows up to 35 feet high [7]. It has circular twigs covered with fine velvety hairs, giving the tree its name [16]. Its leaves are composed of five to nine lanceolate to elliptic leaflets arranged pinnately on a petiole, ranging from 4–10 inches long [16]. The thick and often serrate leaflets turn lemon yellow in autumn and drop off in winter.

Figure 22. Velvet ash *(Fraxinus velutina)* trees at Ash Meadows

Figure 23. Singleleaf ash *(Fraxinus anomala)* tree

Flower clusters lack petals, but male clusters are conspicuous by their bright yellow stamens [7]. In summer, dense clusters of winged fruits (samaras) appear. Each fruit contains a single small seed about the size and shape of a rice grain, with a narrow, green papery wing about 1 inch long attached to one end. Velvet ash is found around springs and streams at Ash Meadows,

Figure 24. Fruits (samaras) of singleleaf ash (*Fraxinus anomala*)

where it grows with screwbean mesquite. It also grows in the Spring Range and on the margins of the Mojave Desert in stream canyons and other mesic locations between 1000 and 4500 feet elevation [5].

Singleleaf ash, unlike velvet ash, is a small tree or large shrub and has nearly square, rather than circular, branchlets. The leaves are typically composed of a single ovate leaflet, although occasionally there may be three leaflets on a leaf; the terminal leaflet is always the largest. Male flower clusters are orange (not yellow, as with velvet ash). The fruit's wing extends all along the body of the flattish (not rounded) seed [7, 16, 41]. Singleleaf ash grows around springs in valley bottoms, in stream canyons and other well-watered habitats in lower mountains, and on relatively dry hillsides at higher elevations up to 11,000 feet [5].

Native Uses

Ash wood is useful for making a variety of tools and utensils. It is straight-grained, strong, and pliable when green, and the wood holds its shape when dried. The Southern Paiute often used ash wood to make the frames of cradleboards [43]. At Ash Meadows, the hard wood was used to make plows in historic times [53]. The Kawaiisu used ash branches to make poles 10 feet or more in length, which they used to knock pinyon pine *(Pinus monophylla)* cones from the trees [87]. Ash wood was favored because it would not break. The Kawaiisu name for ash *(edɨvɨ)* is similar to their term for bow *(edɨ),* suggesting that ash wood was used to make bows. However, the Kawaiisu preferred juniper wood for bowmaking [87]. The Owens Valley Paiute used ash wood to make both bows and pinyon hooks [56].

A crookneck cane or walking stick made of ash wood was recently found in a small cave near Shoshone Mountain, on the Nevada Test Site. These crookneck canes *(pooro* in Chemehuevi) were used as ordinary walking sticks and as hooks to snag down pine branches when collecting pine nuts [46, 50]. Southern Paiute people used such canes to pull desert tortoises out of their burrows [46]. The *pooro* was also "peculiarly the shaman's badge of office," invested with power and sacredness by some Chemehuevi people [50]. Crookneck staffs have been found in various archaeological contexts in the Southwest and Mojave Desert [59, 63].

Sources: [5] Beatley 1976; [7] Benson and Darrow 1981; [16] Cronquist et al. 1984; [41] Hickman 1993; [43] Y. Jake, pers. commun.; [46] Kelly 1932–1934; [50] Laird 1976; [53] C. Lynch, pers. commun.; [56] B. Moose, pers. commun.; [59] Musser-Lopez 1983; [63] Shearin 1990; [87] Zigmond 1981.

Willow Family (Salicaceae)

Sandbar Willow
Salix exigua Nutt.

Figure 25

Owens Valley Paiute: *su'hava* [55, 71]; *suhuva* [65]; *"say-heur-bah"* [49]
Southern Paiute: *kanav* [70, 71]; *kanab* [58]; *kanabɨ* [57];
    kanavɨ, sagah [50]; *"sa-ga-ve"* [53]
Timbisha Shoshone: *"sah-gup," "suh-vee"* [49]
Western Shoshone: *kwishisuuvi* [71]; *"coo-see see-bup," "soo-vee,"*
    "suh-ee-be" [78]; *"kosi tsube"* [58]; *sɨhɨbi* [57]

Goodding's Willow
Salix gooddingii C. Ball

Figure 26

Owens Valley Paiute: *"paseta," "pasidup"* [49]; *"su-ha-vee"* [56]
Southern Paiute: *pawaxanav* [71]

Figure 25. Sandbar
willow *(Salix exigua)*

Timbisha Shoshone: *"kwishi-suuvi"* [25]
Western Shoshone: *suuvi* [71]

Description and Habitat

Sandbar willow (also called narrowleaf willow) is small, 3–6 feet tall, and
often grows in thickets [42]. Its grayish green leaves are 2–5 inches long and
less than 0.5 inch wide [7]. Sandbar willow is widely distributed in moist to
wet soils, and this small willow commonly grows with cottonwood, ash, and
screwbean mesquite. It can also grow in saltbush, blackbrush, sagebrush, and
pinyon-juniper communities, at a range of 2300–8000 feet elevation [5].

Goodding's willow (also known as black willow) is a larger tree, 40–50
feet tall [7, 41], that grows at lower elevations near springs or streams. It has
a thick trunk with coarse blackish bark, yellow twigs on the branches, and
narrow leaves up to 5 inches long [7]. It is typically found at elevations between 3700 and 6200 feet, in association with saltbush, sagebrush, pinyon-juniper woodland, and occasionally, rush *(Juncus)* meadows [5].

Figure 26. Goodding's willow *(Salix gooddingii)*

Native Uses

Young shoots and branches of sandbar willow (or similar species such as arroyo willow, *Salix lasiolepis,* or Pacific willow, *Salix lucida*) were important in the manufacture of baskets, water jugs, cradleboards, and other basketry items [49, 65, 71]. According to many consultants, willow was the most important basketry material in the region. Appropriate stems were cut only in winter [65], before they had sprouted leaves [58]. Stems of black willow were not used for basketry because they were too brittle [87]. To ensure reliable basketry supplies, basketmakers managed their preferred willow stands by selective harvesting, pruning, and burning [33]. Plants were sometimes transplanted to locations near homes so supplies were close at hand [33]. This important resource is still highly prized among modern basketmakers [71].

The stems were peeled before they became too dry, and the peeled bark was carefully made into small coils and saved for use as flexible elements in basketmaking (see figure 27) [58]. The peeled stems were left whole or were split lengthwise to make foundation rods or flexible winding elements. Willow basketmaking materials were often dried and stored for later use. When the basketmaker was ready, she soaked the materials to make them pliable again and began the long process of weaving.

Larger stems or branches of sandbar willow were commonly used to make walls of dwellings [50, 71], and branches of black willow were used as house posts and poles [49]. The Southern Paiute also used willow branches to make the sinew-backed hunting bow and warriors' arrows [48, 50].

Figure 27. Mary Ann Pepo, a Moapa Paiute basketmaker, used specially prepared coils of willow strips to make various utilitarian and decorative baskets. (Photograph courtesy of the Nevada Historical Society, Reno)

Willow had numerous medicinal uses [78]. To relieve pain, the bark was either chewed or boiled to make a tea to obtain the salicylic acid, the active ingredient in aspirin [71]. A tea made from boiled twigs was used for venereal disease, and root-bark tea was a regular spring tonic at Moapa [78]. Charcoal made from willow roots was formed into pills for the treatment of dysentery and influenza. Young twigs steeped in water made a laxative [58], and an excellent physic was produced when these twigs were boiled. Mashed roots applied to the gums eased toothache [78]. An extract from boiled leaves and twigs rubbed into the scalp prevented dandruff.

Sources: [5] Beatley 1976; [7] Benson and Darrow 1981; [25] P. Esteves, pers. commun.; [33] Fowler 1996; [41] Hickman 1993; [42] Jaeger 1941; [48] Kelly 1964; [49] Kerr 1936; [50] Laird 1976; [53] C. Lynch, pers. commun.; [55] V. Miller, pers. commun.; [56] B. Moose, pers. commun.; [57] Mozingo 1987; [58] Murphey 1959; [65] Steward 1933; [70] Stewart 1942; [71] Stoffle et al. 1989; [78] Train et al. 1941; [87] Zigmond 1981.

TREES

Cypress Family (Cupressaceae)

Utah Juniper

Juniperus osteosperma (Torr.) Little

Figures 28–30

Owens Valley Paiute: *hunuvu* [71]; *"hunuve"* [56]
Southern Paiute: *wa'ap* [71]; *"wha-pee," "wah-puee"* [78];
   wa'api (tree), *wapampi* (fruit) [29, 48]; *"pa-wapa," "wampa"* [43]
Timbisha Shoshone: *"sahwavi"* [25]
Western Shoshone: *sanavi* (for *Juniperus scopulorum*) [29, 66];
   sahwavi [71]; *"sahn-ah-poh," "san-ah-bee"* [78]; *wáapi* [29]

Description and Habitat

Utah juniper is an evergreen tree or large shrub, often 10–20 feet high with a broad rounded or open crown; exceptionally large and old individuals may reach 40 feet [17]. The trunk and main branches are clothed in reddish gray fibrous bark, and the stout twigs are covered with bright green scalelike leaves [17]. Twigs bear clusters of reddish brown or bluish berries with a powdery coating. Utah juniper is one of the dominant pygmy conifers in the Great Basin [17] and grows sporadically in the Mojave Desert [7, 41], found in woodlands alone or in combination with sagebrush and pinyon pine on mountain slopes between 5500 and 8000 feet elevation [5].

Figure 28. Utah juniper *(Juniperus osteosperma)*

Figure 29. Utah juniper *(Juniperus osteosperma)* berries

Native Uses

This "very worthy tree" [56] served many uses historically and still does so today. Juniper was a common and popular source of medicine [78]. Young twigs were boiled, often with the berries or other plants thrown in, to make a cold and cough remedy and to treat various other ailments. A boiled decoction of twigs served as an external wash as well. Twigs were ground, moistened, bound up in a cloth, and heated over a fire or with a hot rock; this was held to the throat or jaw for sore throat, swollen jaw, and toothache. Burned twigs were used to clear headaches and colds or to produce sweats for heavy colds. A broth made with boiled berries also had numerous medicinal uses, including treatment for asthma [53, 78]. The leaves and twigs were burned as a ceremonial purifier [71].

Juniper wood was the preferred material for making bows [48, 65]. Juniper trees having trunks with long sections of straight grain were selected, and strips of wood were cut with stone or (in historic times) metal axes. Juniper trees with strips removed to make bowstaves can still be found in southern Nevada (on the Nevada Test Site) and elsewhere [84].

The strong, fine-grained wood was used for fuel and in the construction of houses, sweathouses, shades, windbreaks, fences, and, in historic times, pens and corrals [56, 65, 71]. Juniper wood also served as splints for setting broken bones [47]. Juniper bark or boughs sometimes was used as house-roofing materials [9, 65], and the shredding bark furnished a fiber for making sandals, skirts, rope, and other utilitarian items. The Southern Paiute made a slow match (called *kosovi*) by tightly binding a clump of bark [48].

Figure 30. Utah juniper tree (*Juniperus osteosperma*) with long strips of wood cut from the outer trunk for use in making bows

Punctured seeds formed beads to be strung as necklaces [9, 43, 56, 71]. To make a necklace, seeds were gathered after a rat or squirrel had eaten the outer fruit and chewed a hole in one end of the seed. The partly chewed seeds were washed, dried, and a hole was made in the other end; these were then strung on a cord to make the necklace. Juniper seed necklaces were worn to keep bad spirits away after death [43].

Juniper berries themselves were sometimes eaten [9, 71]. They were gathered in winter and spring, crushed, seeded, and eaten raw [48]. An insect excretion on the tree also served as a food, called *"noo-ahn-tup"* by the Southern Paiute [9].

Utah juniper is important in the modern Native American Church, providing a purifying and sacred smoke for prayers. Juniper smoke is also used to cure buckskin [43].

Sources: [5] Beatley 1976; [7] Benson and Darrow 1981; [9] Bye 1972; [17] Cronquist et al. 1986; [25] P. Esteves, pers. commun.; [29] Fowler 1972; [41] Hickman 1993; [42] Jaeger 1941; [43] Y. Jake, pers. commun.; [48] Kelly 1964; [53] C. Lynch, pers. commun.; [56] B. Moose, pers. commun.; [65] Steward 1933; [66]Steward 1938; [71] Stoffle et al. 1989; [78] Train et al. 1941; [84] Wilke 1988.

Pine Family (Pinaceae)

Singleleaf Pinyon Pine

Pinus monophylla Torr. & Frém.

Figures 31–35

Owens Valley Paiute: *tuvap, tuvah* (nuts) [71]; *tuva'a* [65]; *tuvu, tuvap* [56];
"*son-o-pee*" (pitch) [55]
Southern Paiute: *tuvap, tuvwap* [71]; *tivah* (nuts) [50]; *tövö* (nuts) [70]
Western Shoshone: *wahpi, tuvah* [71]; "*wah-pee*" [78]

Description and Habitat

Singleleaf pinyon is the dominant small pine in mountain areas of the southern Great Basin [17]. It is densely branched, with round needles that grow singly, not in bundles [17]. Its small cones ripen during the fall, sometimes abundantly, bearing a wealth of large pine nuts. Singleleaf pinyon grows on coarse gravelly soils between 5800 and 8500 feet elevation, usually with Utah juniper. Occasionally it is found with white fir and limber pine at upper elevations or with Joshua tree at the lower end of its elevation range [5]. Pinyon trees also grow singly or in scattered clumps as an open steppe-woodland in association with sagebrush.

Native Uses

Pinyon pine was an important all-purpose tree for Native groups in the Great Basin, and it remains very important among Native people today [71].

Figure 31. Singleleaf pinyon pine *(Pinus monophylla)*

TREES

Figure 32. Pinyon pine *(Pinus monophylla)* cones in the green stage, before ripening

Figure 33. Ripened brown pinyon pine *(Pinus monophylla)* cones with exposed seeds

The pine nuts were the "most important plant food" for Great Basin peoples [65, 66, 67]. Individuals, families, and groups of families gathered in good stands of nut-bearing trees during late summer and fall to collect pine nuts [74, 87]. Good crops were irregular, occurring in a given area only once every few years, so families moved from place to place each fall to gather the

Figure 34. Native women gathering pinyon pine nuts (Photograph courtesy of the Nevada Historical Society, Reno)

Figure 35. Removing pinyon pine nuts from the cones (Photograph courtesy of the Nevada Historical Society, Reno)

needed nuts. In some areas, trees were pruned and encouraged to produce good nut crops by beating and thrashing [33, 71]. According to some accounts, individuals gathered thirty to forty bushels of nuts each fall, which were stored for use through the long winter months and into spring [66].

People living at Ash Meadows gathered pine nuts in the Spring Range.

Families gathered on their own tracts, and people rarely trespassed without permission. Pine nuts were gathered until the snow fell. If the Spring Range crop failed, Ash Meadows people often went to Shoshone Peak to gather with Western Shoshone people. Likewise, if the Shoshone Peak crops were bad, Western Shoshone folk were sometimes invited to collect in the Spring Range [66].

Two different collecting methods were used, the most common being the green-cone method [54]. Unripened, green cones were collected in late summer by pulling branches down and plucking off the cones [21]. To release the nuts, cones were opened by steaming or roasting them in a pit over a bed of sagebrush coals [43]. After steaming, the nuts were shaken out and dried on a mat or canvas. Nuts were then rolled lightly on a metate to break the hulls, which were winnowed away and the nutmeats kept.

A second way to collect pine nuts, the brown-cone method [54], was done in autumn as the cones opened. People beat the tree branches with long poles, and the nuts fell onto mats placed around the tree. Nuts were then parched in a tray and hulled as described above, leaving a basketful of nicely toasted nutmeats. Yetta Jake, a Southern Paiute consultant, noted that the nuts cooked in a pit did not keep long and must be eaten or sold soon; nuts gathered from the ground by the brown cone method could be stored through winter [43].

After hulling, nuts were eaten whole or ground into flour to be eaten as meal, a hot or cold mush, or unleavened bread [22, 54, 74]. The nuts are rich in carbohydrates, with lesser amounts of fats and proteins, and yield about 2215 calories per pound [26]. Collecting experiments suggest that the energy return rate for pinyon nuts ranges between 840 and 1400 calories per hour collecting and processing, a relatively high value for plant foods [65].

A clear insect-derived sugar sometimes found on pinyon pine was said to be better than honey [49]. The Timbisha called this pinyon sugar *"wa-pea-harvey"* and used it as a physic [49]. The inner bark of pinyon trees sometimes was eaten during periods of severe want [9].

Pine pitch was also an important medicinal remedy, especially for colds [78]. The resin was boiled to make a hot tea, often in combination with other plants (such as juniper twigs, sagebrush, or purple sage) to increase palatability. People drank the tea for many ailments [78]. Heated resin was used to draw out slivers, cure external wounds, or make a hot plaster for various internal pains and congestion. The pitch was steamed and used as a vaporizer to clear the lungs [25]. Women who desired no more children sometimes drank cooked pinyon pitch [87].

Pine pitch also served as a waterproofing agent for baskets and water jugs, and was used as an adhesive, mortar, sealant, and chewing gum [71]. A finer-grade pitch was used for chewing, whereas a coarser grade was used for mending and as an adhesive, cement, and waterproofing agent [9, 87].

Pinyon wood served as fuel [9] and construction material [71]. The Timbisha made wooden mortars from pinyon wood [87]. Children pinched partly cracked pine nut hulls onto their ears as ornaments [87].

Sources: [5] Beatley 1976; [9] Bye 1972; [17] Cronquist et al. 1986; [21] Dutcher 1893; [22] Ebeling 1986; [25] P. Esteves, pers. commun.; [26] Farris 1980; [33] Fowler 1996; [43] Y. Jake, pers. commun.; [49] Kerr 1936; [50] Laird 1976; [54] Madsen 1986; [55] V. Miller, pers. commun.; [56] B. Moose, pers. commun.; [65] Steward 1933; [66] Steward 1938; [67] Steward 1941; [70] Stewart 1942; [71] Stoffle et al. 1989; [74] Stuart 1945; [78] Train et al. 1941; [87] Zigmond 1981.

Beech Family (Fagaceae)

Gambel's Oak

Quercus gambelii Nutt.

Figure 36, 37

Owens Valley Paiute: *tsiginoh* [71]; "*che-ga-no*" [49];
    "*tosigino*," "*cheigino*" [56]; "*chee-giño*" (scrub oak) [55];
    "*we-ha*" (large acorns) [55]; "*we-ah*" [56]
Southern Paiute: *kwiav* [71]; *kwiavɨ* [48]; *tomömpⁱ* [70];
    tomɨmpi (acorns) [48]

Description and Habitat

Gambel's oak is a small tree or large shrub, usually less than 20 feet tall, with one or more crooked trunks [82]. It often grows clonally, in dense low thickets or in stands of trees with a closed canopy [5]. The leaves are deeply lobed and about 4 inches long. The foliage is yellowish green in the spring, deep green in summer, reddish in autumn, and absent in winter. In summer, the trees produce small acorns, less than 0.75 inch long [82]. Gambel's oak grows along washes, near springs, or on rocky slopes along with sagebrush, pinyon, and juniper between 5400 and 7500 feet elevation [5].

Native Uses

The Owens Valley Paiute procured acorns of the California black oak *(Quercus kelloggii)*, called *we-hah*, from tribes living west of the Sierra Nevada for whom acorns were a staple crop [49, 65]. These large acorns were ground and the bitterness was leached out with running water to make an acorn mush *(coneva)*. Acorns are nutritionally similar to pine nuts—rich in carbohydrates with smaller amounts of fats and proteins—and yield about 2120

Figure 36. Gambel's oak *(Quercus gambelii)*

Figure 37. Gambel's oak
(Quercus gambelii) leaves
and acorns

calories per pound [26]. The long time required to prepare acorns, however, makes their overall caloric return rate fairly low.

Southern Paiute people often ate acorns of Gambel's oak [48]. The Western Shoshone ate them occasionally, as Gambel's oak grows less frequently in their territory. These acorns were not leached, but were roasted in a pit, boiled, and ground into a mush [67, 71]. It is not certain if the acorns of Gambel's oak have a caloric yield similar to that of the California black oak, but the Gambel's oak acorns are smaller and have less edible portion per weight. Consequently, the food utility of Gambel's oak acorns must have been considerably less than the jumbo California acorns.

Oak wood was burned as fuel and in ceremonies. The wood was also used to make spears, bows, canes, and other items [48, 71]. Oak wood is still commonly used for several of these purposes by Native peoples today [71]. The Southern Paiute made paint from a fungus growing on oak trees [48].

Sources: [5] Beatley 1976; [26] Farris 1980; [48] Kelly 1964; [49] Kerr 1936; [55] V. Miller, pers. commun.; [56] B. Moose, pers. commun.; [65] Steward 1933; [67] Steward 1941]; [70] Stewart 1942; [71] Stoffle et al. 1989; [78] Train et al. 1941; [82] Welsh et al. 1987.

Rose Family (Rosaceae)

Curlleaf Mountain Mahogany
Cercocarpus ledifolius Nutt. ex Torr. & Gray

Figures 38, 39

Owens Valley Paiute: *"toobe"* [55, 56]
Southern Paiute: *"tu-nam-ba"* [53]; *"dunumbe"* [58]
Timbisha Shoshone: *"huh-na-vee"* [25]
Western Shoshone: *tünambe* [66]; *"durumbe"* (plant), *"duhul"* (bark) [58]

Description and Habitat

Curlleaf mountain mahogany is a large evergreen shrub or small tree, reaching 25 feet in height, with a sturdy reddish trunk and branches [18]. The leaves are narrow and lanceolate, often with leaf margins rolled in toward the center midrib (hence the name "curlleaf"). The flowers are inconspicuous. The fruit is a small, sharply pointed, rice-shaped seed that bears a long feathery plume [18]. Curlleaf mountain mahogany grows in higher mountains in the region, in association with pinyon pine or sagebrush, from 6000 to 9000 feet elevation [5].

Figure 38. Curlleaf mountain mahogany *(Cercocarpus ledifolius)*

Native Uses

The wood of curlleaf mountain mahogany is extremely hard and durable, ideal for making digging sticks and arrows [66]. The wood was used on the edge of pine nut threshing baskets to make a strong frame [43]. The wood is also an excellent fuel [18], burning hot and smoke-free. The Timbisha used mountain mahogany bark to make twine, rope, mats, or baskets to hold food [25].

The dried bark was an important medicine, especially for pulmonary disorders and the treatment of cuts, sores, burns, and wounds [78]. The bark was dried for two years, after which time it could be used. Once dried, it could be boiled to make a tea for internal use or ground into a powder or paste for external application. A cold tea made of mountain mahogany bark was favored as a blood tonic. Among the Kawaiisu [87], the bark was boiled and the liquid drunk for treatment of gonorrhea. Dried mountain mahogany sap was ground to a powder and used for earaches, and the leaves were boiled with sage to treat rash [25].

Figure 39. Curlleaf mountain mahogany *(Cercocarpus ledifolius)* leaves and plumose flowers

Sources: [5] Beatley 1976; [18] Cronquist et al. 1997; [25] P. Esteves, pers. commun.; [43] Y. Jake, pers. commun.; [53] C. Lynch, pers. commun.; [55] V. Miller, pers. commun.; [56] B. Moose, pers. commun.; [58] Murphey 1959; [66] Steward 1938; [78] Train et al. 1941; [87] Zigmond 1981.

CHAPTER TWO

Large Shrubs and Woody Vines

Sunflower Family (Asteraceae)

Arrowweed
   Pluchea sericea (Nutt.) Cov.

Figures 40, 41

Southern Paiute: *"sah-wape"* [53, 78]; *sawapɨ* [50]
Timbisha Shoshone: *"chavoe," "esha-whoap"* [49]

Figure 40. Arrowweed
(Pluchea sericea)

Figure 41. A Timbisha woman and child sit below a sun shade made of willow poles and arrowweed branches in Death Valley. (Photograph courtesy of U.S. Borax and Chemical Corporation)

Description and Habitat

Arrowweed is a willowlike shrub with long straight branches that grows to 15 feet tall [14, 41]. Its lanceolate leaves are covered with white silky hair, giving them a silvery gray color [14]. The flower heads are pale roseate purple tufts found on branch ends [42]. White-tufted seed heads form after flowering. This shrub forms thickets near springs, saline desert watercourses, and river bottoms, sometimes in pure dense stands [42]. It grows with willow *(Salix)* or bulrush *(Scirpus)* below 3000 feet elevation, in moist areas such as Ash Meadows [5].

Native Uses

The young straight shoots and branches of arrowweed were useful for making arrow shafts [49, 71], as thatching in the construction of houses and shades [50], for making granaries [4, 10], and lining roasting pits [32]. The Southern Paiute name of the plant *("sah-wape")* apparently derives from its use in making arrows, which are called *"sawaj"* [58]. Arrowweed was apparently an important trade item among Paiute women at Ash Meadows [71]. The root was either boiled into a tea or chewed raw to ease indigestion or stop diarrhea [78].

Sources: [4] Bean and Saubel 1972; [5] Beatley 1976; [10] Castetter and Bell 1951; [14] Cronquist 1994; [32] Fowler 1995; [41] Hickman 1993; [42] Jaeger 1941; [49] Kerr 1936; [50] Laird 1976; [53] C. Lynch, pers. commun.; [58] Murphey 1959; [71] Stoffle et al. 1989; [78] Train et al. 1941.

LARGE SHRUBS AND WOODY VINES

Grape Family (Vitaceae)

Canyon Grape
Vitis arizonica Engelm.

Figure 42

Owens Valley Paiute: *"ovus," "ea-deave-sa-nucca"* [49]; *"sa-nucca"* [56]
Southern Paiute: *i'av, kuripsup* [71]; *iyaavi* (fruit) [50];
  iyaavimpɨ (plant) [50, 52]
Timbisha Shoshone: *"eshah-wah-nup," "eshah-sham-bu," "sham-boop"* [49];
  muvasi [25]
Western Shoshone: *muvasi* [71]

Description and Habitat

Canyon grape is a large woody vine with climbing or trailing branches [18].
It has maplelike leaves, shreddy bark, and coiling tendrils [7]. Inconspicuous
white flowers bloom in the spring and turn into dark blue, juicy fruit in late
summer and fall. Wild grape grows in wet to moist soils near springs, such as

Figure 42. Canyon grape
(Vitis arizonica) vines and
fruits

at Ash Meadows, where it is common. It is associated with ash, screwbean mesquite, and saltbush between 2200 and 5000 feet elevation [5].

Native Uses

Grapes were eaten raw or dried, and stored for year-round consumption [9, 71]. They were also cooked [49], and one source suggests that Great Basin peoples made grape jelly and wine [71]. The seeds were saved and ground up for various food uses [9]. The vines were useful for tying saplings together in house construction [50]. Grapevines were encouraged and managed, and seeds were planted in different locations to widen their distribution [71]. In the 1870s, Southern Paiute people marketed wild grapes to White settlers as a cash crop [9].

Sources: [5] Beatley 1976; [7] Benson and Darrow 1981; [9] Bye 1972; [18] Cronquist et al. 1997; [25] P. Esteves, pers. commun.; [49] Kerr 1936; [50] Laird 1976; [52] Lawlor 1995; [56] B. Moose, pers. commun.; [71] Stoffle et al. 1989.

Caltrop Family (Zygophyllaceae)

Creosote Bush, *Larrea tridentata* (DC) Cov.

Figures 43, 44

Owens Valley Paiute: *"yer-up," "ge-a-more-up"* [49]
Southern Paiute: *yatamp, yatumb* [71]; *yatampɨ* [50, 87]; *ya'tam'pi* [47]; *yatumbi* [53]; *"ya-temp"* [58]; *"tah-sup-up"* [9]
Timbisha Shoshone: *"yah-tam-vee"* [49]; *"ya tombe"* [58]
Western Shoshone: *yatumbi* [71]

Description and Habitat

Creosote bush is a dominant shrub over vast areas of the Mojave Desert and is one of the characteristic plants of many Mojave Desert plant communities between 2200 and 5200 feet elevation [7, 42]. It is a multistemmed, spreading shrub that grows 2–10 feet high [18, 41]. Black rings mark its slender branches. The branches bear sprays of small yellowish green leaves, which are clustered in pairs of leaflets. The leaflets are oval with an acute tip and are resinous, imparting a characteristic creosote-like aroma. Bright yellow flowers bloom in April and May and occasionally in late summer, if there is sufficient rain. Silver-furred fruits, each composed of five nutlets, follow the flowers. Some shrubs grow in clonal clusters that may be more than 11,000 years old [80], making creosote bush one of the longest-lived plants known (although individual shrubs do not live this long).

LARGE SHRUBS AND WOODY VINES

Figure 43. Creosote bush *(Larrea tridentata)*

Figure 44. Creosote bush *(Larrea tridentata)* flowers and furry seeds

Native Uses

This ubiquitous shrub of the Mojave Desert had many uses and it has been ranked as among the most important of plants by Native groups [72]. The wood was burned for fuel. Branches were used to build summer shades against the desert heat and to make digging sticks, tool handles, and other utilitarian articles. The lac, a sticky exudate made by insects, was an important glue, binding agent, and sealant [9, 71, 87]. Creosote bush lac has been identified on archaeological arrow and spear points and knives, indicating that it was commonly used to hold the stone tool or bone awl in its haft [35, 76]. Lac was also used to mend pottery and to waterproof baskets [87]. Creosote bush is the most favored source of remedies for Native peoples in the southern Great Basin [71, 78]. According to Carobeth Laird [50], creosote bush "was and is one of the great medicinal plants of the Chemehuevis. It is classified as *navuʷaganumpɨ*... a substance which ordinary folk apply to themselves or to others," without involving the healing skills of a shaman. The Southern Paiute consider the plant to be a cure-all, with various teas, formulas, and baths devised to help measles especially [47], but also rheumatism, cramps, chicken pox, sores, venereal disease, and (mixed with badger oil) a salve for burns [78]. The Beatty Shoshone people made a tea from boiled leaves to cure venereal disease and colds and to stimulate urination [78]. A lotion made from the plant was used to treat sores on people and animals. Powdered leaves were also applied to sores; the lac acted as a styptic [9]. The Timbisha boiled the leaves in Coso Hot Springs water and used it as a liniment, and a tea made of the leaves was a good stomach medicine [49] or relieved cramps [58]. Some people bathe in the liquid to relieve body aches, and some say that leaves heated on a fire and covered with dirt could relieve aching body parts placed over the mound [87]. The leaves also were burned during religious observances [71].

Creosote bush is still highly regarded as a medicinal plant by people today. Several consultants reported that a tea of the leaves was useful in curing cancer [55, 71]. Experimental tests of its cancer-curing properties have given inconsistent and contradictory results, however, and recent cases of liver damage have been attributed to internal use of creosote bush [77]. Therefore, its use as an internal medicine is strongly discouraged.

Sources: [7] Benson and Darrow 1981; [9] Bye 1972; [18] Cronquist et al. 1997; [35] Fox et al. 1995; [41] Hickman 1993; [42] Jaeger 1941; [49] Kerr 1936; [50] Laird 1976; [53] C. Lynch, pers. commun.; [55] V. Miller, pers. commun.; [58] Murphey 1959; [71] Stoffle et al. 1989; [72] Stoffle et al. 1990; [76] Sutton 1990; [77] Tilford 1997; [78] Train et al. 1941; [80] Vasek 1980; [87] Zigmond 1981.

Goosefoot Family (Chenopodiaceae)

Fourwing Saltbush
Atriplex canescens (Pursh) Nutt.

Figure 45

LARGE SHRUBS AND WOODY VINES

Figure 45. Fourwing saltbush *(Atriplex canescens)*

Owens Valley Paiute: *tonoh* [71]; *"to-nah"* [56]; *to'nova* [65]
Southern Paiute: *"que-ahe-que"* [9]; *"ova-va-na-ha-ve"* [53]; *murunib[i]* [47]
Western Shoshone: *"moo-roon-up"* [78]

Description and Habitat

Fourwing saltbush is an erect woody shrub, 2–4 feet high, with intricately branched, scurfy twigs and small, pale grayish green, elongated leaves [7, 41]. The inconspicuous flowers become clusters of pale green fruits, each with four distinctive wings growing out of the central axis, where the seed is located [57]. Fourwing saltbush is common in several plant communities in the southern Great Basin below about 7500 feet elevation. It is one of the most consistently found species in the transition zone between the Mojave Desert and Great Basin floristic regions [5, 7].

Native Uses

The hard wood of this shrub was used for firewood and to make arrows and arrowheads [55, 71, 87]. One source indicates that the seeds were used for food by Southern Paiute people [87], but the use of seeds as food was denied by Owens Valley Paiute [65]. Fresh roots were boiled with a little salt to make a general physic [78]. Southern Paiute people rubbed sores with the leaves as a healing agent.

Sources: [5] Beatley 1976; [7] Benson and Darrow 1981; [9] Bye 1972; [41] Hickman 1993; [47] Kelly 1939; [53] C. Lynch, pers. commun.; [55] V. Miller, pers. commun.; [56] B. Moose, pers. commun; [57] Mozingo 1987; [65] Steward 1933; [71] Stoffle et al. 1989; [78] Train et al. 1941; [87] Zigmond 1981.

Goosefoot Family (Chenopodiaceae)

Shadscale

Atriplex confertifolia (Torr. & Frém.) S. Wats.

Figures 46, 47

Southern Paiute: *kakumb* [71]; *"que-ahe-que"* [9]; *"kakumba"* [53]

Description and Habitat

Shadscale is a large woody shrub; its canopy may grow up to 4 feet in diameter, with a maze of zigzagging twigs that often having spiny tips [7, 41, 57]. The pale grayish green scurfy leaves may drop during drought, leaving the twigs exposed [57]. The flowers are inconspicuous. The small fruits are roughly triangular, with two leaflike wings arising from a basal seed pocket. Shadscale is very common in many plant communities; indeed this plant is "probably the most abundant shrub of the region" [5]. It is especially common in areas where soils are heavily textured and slightly salty, where it may grow in pure stands.

Figure 46. Shadscale *(Atriplex confertifolia)*

Native Uses

New fresh leaves were used as a poultice or powder to heal cuts. The plant is still used today for medicinal purposes [71]. The wood was burned for fuel [9, 71]. Seeds were sometimes eaten by the Southern Paiute [9].

Sources: [5] Beatley 1976; [7] Benson and Darrow 1981; [9] Bye 1972; [53] C. Lynch, pers. commun.; [57] Mozingo 1987; [71] Stoffle et al. 1989.

Figure 47. Shadscale *(Atriplex confertifolia)* twigs and green papery fruits

---

Goosefoot Family (Chenopodiaceae)

Greasewood

Sarcobatus vermiculatus (Hook.) Torr.

Figures 48, 49

Southern Paiute: *tonovi* [57]
Western Shoshone: *tonovi* [66]; *tonobi* [57]

Description and Habitat

Greasewood is a large woody shrub that grows to 5 feet high, with intricate spine-tipped, whitish twigs, dark gray branches, and bright green succulent leaves [7]. It is found in valley bottoms and around playa edges, where its salt tolerance allows it to thrive where most other plants cannot. Greasewood is most common in the cool-desert Great Basin, less so in the warmer Mojave Desert [5, 7].

Figure 48. Greasewood *(Sarcobatus vermiculatus)*

Figure 49. Greasewood *(Sarcobatus vermiculatus)* foliage and male conelike flower clusters

Native Uses

The tough branches of greasewood served well for making digging sticks, arrow foreshafts, arrow points, cradleboard and basket edges, and other items requiring hard wood [43, 48, 67]. The Southern Paiute occasionally used the seeds for food [9].

Sources: [5] Beatley 1976; [7] Benson and Darrow 1981; [9] Bye 1972; [43] Y. Jake, pers. commun.; [48] Kelly 1964; [57] Mozingo 1987; [66] Steward 1938; [67] Steward 1941.

Nightshade Family (Solanaceae)
Anderson's Wolfberry
Lycium andersonii Gray

Figures 50, 51

Owens Valley Paiute: *huupia* [71]; *"hoop-e-wah"* [49]; *"hun-ipee"* [55]
Southern Paiute: *pa'up, u'up, hu'up* [71]; *hu'upiva* [66]; *"hoop-pi-ve"* (bush), *"hupoo"* (berries) [53]; *"u-ope"* [9]; *hu'upi* [50]; *u'upɨ* [48]
Timbisha Shoshone: *"whoo-pee-ah," "whoo-pea"* [49]
Western Shoshone: *huupi* [71]

Description and Habitat

Anderson's wolfberry (also known as tomato berry or desert thorn) is a thorny shrub growing up to 10 feet in height, with many stout zigzagging

Figure 50. Anderson's wolfberry *(Lycium andersonii)*

Figure 51. Anderson's wolfberry *(Lycium andersonii)* fruits

branchlets. It has small, succulent, sausage-shaped leaves and light lavender
flowers [7, 16, 41]. The berries are small and tomato red. Anderson's wolfberry is widely distributed throughout Arizona and southern Nevada at elevations of less than 6000 feet [5, 7]. It is common on gravelly or rocky
slopes and in washes and is most commonly associated with creosote bush,
spiny hopsage, and blackbrush [5].

Native Uses

The red berries of Anderson's wolfberry were prized as a food and juice
source [9, 71], particularly by the Southern Paiute [9, 31, 50], who considered it "the best berry of all" [48]. Hand-picking the berries was very difficult due to the plant's thorns [50]. The berries, gathered in early spring,
were beaten into a basket with a stick [50]; they could be eaten fresh or as
juice or they could be dried whole or mashed [87]. Once dried, they were
eaten raw or reconstituted by soaking or boiling in water [49, 87]. Mashed
berries might also be ground to a powder and made into a paste [49, 87].
Dried berries, either whole or crushed, were stored for year-round consumption, much like other berries. They could be kept for several years when
dried [53]. Berries from varieties of this plant are still in use today [71].

Sources: [5] Beatley 1976; [7] Benson and Darrow 1981; [9] Bye 1972; [16] Cronquist et al. 1984; [31] Fowler 1986; [41] Hickman 1993; [48] Kelly 1964; [49] Kerr
1936; [50] Laird 1976; [53] C. Lynch, pers. commun.; [55] V. Miller, pers. commun.; [66] Steward 1938; [71] Stoffle et al. 1989; [87] Zigmond 1981.

Pea Family (Fabaceae)

Nevada Smokebush

Psorothamnus polydenius (Torr. ex S. Wats.) Rydb.

Figure 52

Owens Valley Paiute: *"cuy-utsie"* [49]
Western Shoshone: *muipuh* [71]; *"mah-good-tu-hoo,"*
"moh-goon-du-hu" [78]

Fremont's Dalea

Psorothamnus fremontii (Torr. ex Gray) Barneby

Figure 53

Owens Valley Paiute: *"cuy-utsie"* [56]
Southern Paiute: *"i-era-midja"* [78]; *"po-heda-watu"* [49]
Western Shoshone: *"quee-um-be,"* *"tuh-goo-buss-e-emp"* [78]

Description and Habitat

Nevada smokebush (also called dotted dalea) is a shrub ranging up to 5 feet in height, with angular stiff stems bearing few leaves [1, 41]. The smaller stems taper to spine-tipped ends and have tiny leaves that usually fall off in the summer [57]. Yellowish orange pinhead-sized glands scattered over its light green stems give off a subtle fragrance. The clusters of pea-shaped flowers are deep pinkish purple [41]. Nevada smokebush grows in loose sand, talus slopes, and tuff conglomerate outcrops, in association with fourwing

Figure 52. Nevada smokebush *(Psorothamnus polydenia)* flowers and dotted branches

Figure 53. Fremont's dalea *(Psorothamnus fremontii)*

saltbush, wolfberry, spiny hopsage, and big sagebrush. It is found between 3500 and 5500 feet elevation [5].

Fremont's dalea (also known as indigo bush) is similar in appearance to Nevada smokebush but smaller, usually less than 3 feet high, with more silvery foliage [1, 41]. Its flowers grow in elongated deep purple clusters. Fremont's dalea is found on limestone and volcanic slopes, commonly in association with Mojave Desert shrubs such as creosote bush, saltbush, white burrobush, wolfberry, and blackbrush, below 4400 feet elevation [5].

Native Uses

The flowers of Nevada smokebush were a well-known remedy for colds and coughs [78]. A tea was made from boiling or steeping fresh or dried stems. Pneumonia, influenza, tuberculosis, and a wide variety of other ailments were also treated with this tea. The flowers were mixed with native tobacco for smoking [71]. According to some sources, the plant is still used today for these purposes [43, 71]. Nevada smokebush seeds were also ground and eaten [49].

Roots and tops of Fremont's dalea were boiled to make a tea to stop internal hemorrhages or stomach trouble [78]. The leaves, flowers, and stems were cooked, and the resulting liquid was used as a beverage [49].

Sources: [1] Barneby 1989; [5] Beatley 1976; [41] Hickman 1993; [43] Y. Jake, pers. commun.; [49] Kerr 1936; [56] B. Moose, pers. commun; [57] Mozingo 1987; [71] Stoffle et al. 1989; [78] Train et al. 1941.

LARGE SHRUBS AND WOODY VINES

Ephedra Family (Ephedraceae)

Nevada Jointfir
Ephedra nevadensis S. Wats.

Green Mormon Tea
Ephedra viridis Cov.

Figures 54–56

Owens Valley Paiute: *turup* [71]; *"to-loop-toiya,"* *"too-loop"* (for *Ephedra viridis*) [49]; *"to-loop-na-pussy"* (for *Ephedra nevadensis*) [49]
Southern Paiute: *yatup* [71]; *utupi* [48]; *tutupi* [57];
    "tu-tupe" [78]; *tu-tupi* [47]
Timbisha Shoshone: *"to-tombe,"* *"tew-tumbe"* [49]
Western Shoshone: *tutumbi, tutupi, u'tuup* [71]; *tudumbi* [57];
    tut'mbip [66]; *"coo-see too-roombe,"* *"too-roombe,"* *"too-toombe"* [78]

Description and Habitat

These two species are broomlike shrubs that grow to about 3 feet high and nearly as wide or wider; they have jointed green or yellowish green stems and tiny scalelike leaves arranged in twos or threes at each joint [17]. The shrubs bear male and female cones that resemble small flowers, but are not true flowers [7, 17]. Named from the Greek for the horsetail plant, which it superficially resembles, *Ephedra* is an ancient member of the gymnosperms, distantly related to pines and other conifers [42].

Nevada jointfir is marked by its grayish green or brownish green color

Figure 54. Nevada jointfir *(Ephedra nevadensis)* in flower

Figure 55. Green Mormon tea *(Ephedra viridis)*, female plant

Figure 56. Green Mormon tea *(Ephedra viridis)*, male flowers

[17, 57]. The spreading, divergent branches are stout, with two scalelike leaves at each joint. It inhabits drier habitats than green Mormon tea and is common in the rocky soils of arid regions throughout the desert Southwest. Nevada jointfir (also known as gray Mormon tea) grows in association with creosote bush, bud sagebrush *(Artemisia spinescens)*, wolfberry, blackbrush, and sagebrush between 2000 and 6000 feet elevation [5].

Green Mormon tea is bright green or yellowish green, with numerous slender parallel branches pointing upward [17, 57]. Like Nevada jointfir, it has two scalelike leaves at each joint. Green Mormon tea is common in sage-brush and pinyon-juniper zones between 4500 and 7500 feet elevation in the southwestern and Great Basin deserts [5].

Native Uses

Native Americans of the region know Mormon tea as "Indian tea," because they used it before the latter-day settlers, and they still drink it frequently today [71]. Many groups use the stems to make a refreshing beverage. Gray ephedra tea is bitterer than the preferred green ephedra tea.

The medicinal qualities of the tea were well known, and it was used to treat a variety of ailments [78], especially stomach, kidney, and other internal disorders [47, 49, 66]. Tea made from Nevada jointfir was used to treat venereal disease or stimulate urination. For the former treatment, ballhead gilia *(Ipomopsis congesta)* was sometimes added to the tea to compound the effect [9, 78]. Green Mormon tea was also used for treating venereal disease, sometimes combining antelope bitterbrush *(Purshia tridentata)* bark or sky-rocket gilia *(Ipomopsis aggregata)* plants [78]. It was also used for the treatment of bladder disorders, colds, and backaches and as a blood purifier. The Kawaiisu drank ephedra tea to alleviate back pain [87]. For a physic, the stems or roots were boiled in salt water. Dried and pulverized stems were applied to sores either as a powder or, mixed with pine pitch, as a salve [78].

Ephedra seeds were parched for eating by some groups, including the Owens Valley Paiute [49] and Timbisha [12, 66]. Frederick Coville [12] noted the Timbisha ground the seeds and made bread from the flour. Roots were ground for chewing gum [49]. Ephedra charcoal was the best kind for making tattoos, which were applied with a horsebrush *(Tetradymia)* spine [87].

Sources: [5] Beatley 1976; [7] Benson and Darrow 1981; [9] Bye 1972; [12] Coville 1892; [17] Cronquist et al. 1986; [42] Jaeger 1941; [47] Kelly 1939; [48] Kelly 1964; [49] Kerr 1936; [57] Mozingo 1987; [66] Steward 1938; [71] Stoffle et al. 1989; [78] Train et al. 1941.

Sunflower Family (Asteraceae)

Rubber Rabbitbrush
Ericameria nauseosa (Pallas ex Pursh) Nesom & Baird

Figure 57

Owens Valley Paiute: *"sea-goop"* [49]; *"sea-kum"* [55]; *"se-goo-pe"* [56]
Southern Paiute: *sikump, s'kump, wa'arump* [71]; *sögumpö* [70]; *sikimpi* [57]; *skumpi* [48]

Western Shoshone: *sipümb, toyaziwɔp* [66]; *sibupi* [57];
"*tah-bah-she-up*," "*see-bape*" [78]

Description and Habitat

The rabbitbrushes are a complex group of shrubs that botanists group into two closely related genera, *Ericameria* and *Chrysothamnus*, with a wide variety of species and subspecies. The shrubs are usually densely branched and round-topped and grow to about 2–4 feet high; the leaves are narrow, green to grayish green, and 1–2 inches long [14, 57]. The shrubs are covered with bright yellow flowers in late summer and fall. Rubber rabbitbrush gets its name from the high rubber content in its foliage [42]. Rabbitbrush is most commonly found in sandy or disturbed soils, especially along washes. Rubber rabbitbrush can be found in blackbrush, shadscale, sagebrush, and pinyon-juniper associations and occasionally with creosote bush scrub [5].

Native Uses

Rabbitbrush leaves were steeped as a tea for stomach disorders and colds. The tops and roots were also boiled to make a tea for coughs, colds, and other ailments [78]. A tea made from the related species green rabbitbrush (*Chrysothamnus viscidiflorus*) was also used for coughs and colds, and the leaves were mashed as a poultice for rheumatism [78]. Another species, called *pasawitümb:* by the Western Shoshone, was used as a liniment made from boiling the whole plant [66].

A chewing gum was made from rabbitbrush roots [49]. The Owens Valley

Figure 57. Rubber rabbitbrush *(Ericameria nauseosa)*

LARGE SHRUBS AND WOODY VINES

Paiute colored the gum with tiger lily *(Lilium lancifolium)* petals. The Kawaiisu threaded pine nuts onto a sharpened, stripped twig of rabbitbrush to improve the nuts' flavor [87].

Branches served as roofing materials for brush lodges [71] and were used to apply pitch to water jugs [48]. The bright yellow blooms in late summer signaled that pine nuts were ready to harvest in the mountains [43, 53]. Today, elders use the flowers for funeral bouquets [56].

Sources: [14] Cronquist 1994; [42] Jaeger 1941; [43] Y. Jake, pers. commun.; [48] Kelly 1964; [49] Kerr 1936; [53] C. Lynch, pers. commun.; [55] V. Miller, pers. commun.; [56] B. Moose, pers. commun.; [57] Mozingo 1987; [66] Steward 1938; [70] Stewart 1942; [71] Stoffle et al. 1989; [78] Train et al. 1941; [87] Zigmond 1981.

Sunflower Family (Asteraceae)

Big Sagebrush
Artemisia tridentata Nutt.

Figure 58

Owens Valley Paiute: *sawava, sawavuᵛᵃ* [65];
  "*sow-wa-bah,*" "*sow-ah-we-ha*" [49]; "*sawabe*" [55]
Southern Paiute: *saŋwav* [71]; *saŋwabi* [57]; *saŋwavi* [48]; "*sa-wa-ve*" [53]; *sawa'bü* [66]; *sawak* [58]
Western Shoshone: *povi, pohovi* [71]; *bohovi* [66]; *pohobi* [57]

Description and Habitat

Big sagebrush is the characteristic shrub of the cool Great Basin desert, dominating hundreds of square miles of sandy valley floors and plains above approximately 5000 feet elevation [5, 57]. Individual shrubs are generally rounded to spreading in outline and 2–10 feet high; the twisted, sinuous branches have fibrous bark and wood that flakes off in strips [14]. The leaves are narrow and wedge shaped, with three small lobes at the end and a hairy surface that gives them a bluish to greenish gray color [14]. The small inconspicuous flowers are borne on slender vertical stems that rise above the leafy shrub in late summer. The penetrating smell of sagebrush filling the air after a summer thunderstorm is an unforgettable Great Basin desert experience.

Native Uses

Big sagebrush was a medicinal plant of major importance [78]. Green leaves and tops were boiled to make a hot or cold tea or sometimes were chewed

Figure 58. Big sagebrush *(Artemisia tridentata)*

raw to relieve a variety of ailments, including stomach disorders, headaches, coughs, colds, sore eyes, and worms [9, 47, 65, 66]. Ground-up leaves were applied to scars resulting from smallpox or chicken pox to remove them [43]. A tea helped produce sweating during fever and was used as an antiseptic wash. Newborns were bathed in a warm decoction of leaves. Steam from boiled leaves was inhaled for relief of colds or headache. Boiled leaves could also be used as a poultice for cuts and bruises. A menstruating woman used a sagebrush stick as a head-scratcher because "any other kind of wood would cause the hair to fall out and the face to wrinkle" [87].

Sagebrush branches were burned after an illness as a fumigant; baskets and blankets used during childbirth were held in the smoke. Leaves were burned in the fire or puffed in pipes to create a fragrant and purifying smoke in sweatlodges, at ceremonial gatherings, and funerals. The ashes were sometimes smudged onto walls of houses or other structures in an act of purification [71]. Sagebrush is still used for these purposes by Native people today [71].

Sagebrush was also an important source of raw materials for manufacturing a variety of wooden articles and textiles. Sagebrush was specially selected to make fire-starting equipment. Fire hearths equipped with several holes were constructed of flat pieces of sagebrush wood, and the drill used to create the friction was fitted with a sagebrush wood foreshaft into a piece of cane [87]. Shredded sagebrush bark was placed next to the fire hearth holes to catch and hold the spark. According to anthropologist Julian Steward [65], "Special individuals with supernatural powers made these; one without the power could not even make himself one which would work." Sagebrush bark was also used to make twined rope, bags, and garments, especially in the northern Great Basin [66]. Pounded bark served as a lining for winter shoes, and strips of bark were bunched together to cork basketry water jugs [87]. A pitchlike lac substance found on sagebrush was collected and shaped into handles for awls and stone knives or used to glue awls and knives into wooden handles [87]. The Southern Paiute used big sagebrush as a dye [9].

Sagebrush wood was also commonly used as a fuel, especially in treeless areas. It was the common fuel for pit-roasting pinyon cones [43, 53]. "In the roasting of pinyons," wrote Maurice Zigmond of the Kawaiisu, "*sohovi* and pinyon-tree *(Pinus monophylla)* wood are specified for the firing. The use of *sohovi* enables the seeds 'to come out easily' " [87]. Sagebrush wood was not used to pit-roast yucca, however, because it made the yucca hearts taste bitter [87]. Sagebrush seeds, thrown into the campfire, would "explode like firecrackers" [87].

Use of sagebrush seeds as food was a matter of taste. According to Julian Steward's consultants, sagebrush seeds were bitter and unpalatable, but they were sometimes mixed with other seeds to stretch the food supply in times of want [65, 66]. There are also reports, however, that the ground seeds were eaten plain or mixed with other seeds or meal "to improve the flavor" [49]. The tiny blossoms are occasionally used to flavor wheat flour.

Sources: [5] Beatley 1976; [9] Bye 1972; [14] Cronquist 1994; [43] Y. Jake, pers. commun.; [48] Kelly 1964; [49] Kerr 1936; [53] C. Lynch, pers. commun.; [55] V. Miller, pers. commun.; [57] Mozingo 1987; [58] Murphey 1959; [65] Steward 1933; [66] Steward 1938; [71] Stoffle et al. 1989; [78] Train et al. 1941; [87] Zigmond 1981.

Rose Family (Rosaceae)
Stansbury Cliffrose
Purshia stansburiana (Torr.) Henrickson

Desert Bitterbrush
Purshia glandulosa Curran

Figures 59–61

Owens Valley Paiute: *"unip"* [55]
Southern Paiute: *u'nup* [71]; *"hunupi"* [53]; *ina'pi* [47]
Western Shoshone: *hunavi* [71]; *hinabi* [57]; *hünabⁱ* [66]; *"her-na-vea"* [49]; *"huh-nabbe," "linna-huh-nabbe"* [78]

Figure 59. Desert bitterbrush *(Purshia glandulosa)*

Figure 60. Desert bitterbrush *(Purshia glandulosa)* flowers

Description and Habitat

Stansbury cliffrose and desert bitterbrush are two closely related species. They grow as large shrubs to small trees that are up to 12 feet tall. These shrubs have irregularly branched trunks with grayish brown, fibrous bark [18, 41, 57]. Small evergreen leaves grow in clusters on the branchlets. The

LARGE SHRUBS AND WOODY VINES

Figure 61. Cliffrose *(Purshia stansburiana)* covered with feathery fruits

leaves are wedge shaped and deeply incised into lobes at their tips. Leaves of Stansbury cliffrose typically have five to nine deep lobes with fine hairs beneath. In spring, cliffrose bears abundant showy white to cream five-petaled flowers, which mature to fruits (achenes) bearing long feathery plumes. Desert bitterbrush, in contrast, has leaves that are glandular, somewhat sticky, and divided into three to five lobes [18, 57]. The glandular leaves of desert bitterbrush distinguish it from a closely related shrub, antelope bitterbrush *(Purshia tridentata)*, which commonly grows in the Great Basin to the north [57]. The yellow or cream-colored flowers of desert bitterbrush are smaller and less showy than those of cliffrose. The fruits are conical and taper to a beak, rather than a plume. Stansbury cliffrose is highly conspicuous in flower and fruit, growing widely in blackbrush, sagebrush, and sagebrush-pinyon communities in the mountains of the region at 4200–7000 feet elevation [5]. Desert bitterbrush is common in washes and slopes between 3200 and 6000 feet elevation, where it grows in blackbrush, spiny hopsage, wolfberry, saltbush, and sagebrush communities [5].

Native Uses

The shreddy bark of bitterbrush and cliffrose was an important fiber source [9, 43, 48] used to make a variety of items including diapers, rope, string, skirts, sandals, infant blankets, and "house crosses for protection against thunder and lightning" [71]. Mats made of the bark (called *"when-o-nabe"* by the Owens Valley Paiute), were used to line food caches to keep out vermin [55]. The bark also had ceremonial uses and served as a medicinal poultice. The wood was a valuable fuel as well [53]. Cooking the ripe seeds yields a beautiful violet dye [58]. The plants remain in use today [71].

Leaves of bitterbrush and cliffrose were often boiled as a tea or antiseptic wash, in a variety of preparations and treatments, to cure or relieve smallpox and measles [78]. Sometimes the tea would be combined with pinyon pine pitch or with crushed lichens and dried woodrat urine (called *"kah-seep"*) [78]. The boiled leaves, stems, roots, or inner bark also made a tea widely used to cure venereal disease, colds, and back pains or used as an emetic, physic, or laxative [49, 78, 87]. The golden tea is strong and sour.

Sources: [5] Beatley 1976; [9] Bye 1972; [18] Cronquist et al. 1997; [41] Hickman 1993; [43] Y. Jake, pers. commun.; [48] Kelly 1964; [49] Kerr 1936; [53] C. Lynch, pers. commun.; [55] V. Miller, pers. commun.; [57] Mozingo 1987; [58] Murphey 1959; [71] Stoffle et al. 1989; [78] Train et al. 1941; [87] Zigmond 1981.

Sumac Family (Anacardiaceae)

Skunkbush Sumac
Rhus trilobata Nutt.

Figures 62, 63

Southern Paiute: *su'uv* [71]; *"see-a-wimp"* [58, 78]; *i'iši, si'ibi* [57]; *siiwimpi* [48]; *siövi* (bush), *i'is* (berries) [70]; *"soo-hoo-vimp"* [79]; *sihivimp* [51]; *"eissia"* (berries), *"suh-vamp"* (bush) [53]

Description and Habitat

Skunkbush sumac is a spreading shrub that generally grows to 3–10 feet tall and as broad or broader [18, 57]. Its stems are slender and arched, with smooth brown bark. The leaves are deeply lobed and compound, composed of three leaflets. They are wedge shaped, shiny, and smooth or velvety [18]. Small yellow flowers, clustered at the ends of branches, mature to become tart reddish orange fruits. Skunkbush sumac inhabits dry, rocky slopes, cliff faces, and occasionally moist valley bottoms [57]. It is found occasionally in mountainous areas in sagebrush and lower pinyon-juniper communities, from 4800 to 6600 feet elevation; it is also found associated with sagebrush and blackbrush in washes at lower elevations [5].

Native Uses

Young branches of skunkbush sumac were (and are) highly esteemed by Southern Paiute basketmakers [48, 71] as the preferred material for cradle-

Figure 62. Skunkbush sumac *(Rhus trilobata)*

Figure 63. Skunkbush sumac *(Rhus trilobata)* fruits

boards, winnowing trays, and other kinds of baskets. Skunkbush sumac was considered superior to willow, another important basketmaking material [48]. To encourage ideal growth of new shoots for basketry, plants were managed by transplanting, pruning, and burning to stimulate growth. Split stems were used much like willow, but unsplit stems of skunkbush sumac could not be used as warps in twined basketry because they are too short [87]. Stems for making baskets were stored for year-round use. Southern Paiute artisans still value this shrub highly and view it as becoming increasingly rare [71]. Southern Paiute people in Utah use it today to make wedding baskets, which are sought for purchase by Navajo medicine men and by collectors of Native American craft.

When stems and leaves were boiled together with pinyon pitch and yellow ochre, an excellent black dye was produced. This dye could be used to color basketry materials, buckskin, feathers, or (in historic times) wool [58].

The red fruits were eaten fresh or dried or ground and drunk as a beverage [9, 57]. Dried fruits were stored for year-round use.

Sources: [5] Beatley 1976; [9] Bye 1972; [18] Cronquist et al. 1997; [48] Kelly 1964; [51] Laird 1984; [53] C. Lynch, pers. commun.; [57] Mozingo 1987; [58] Murphey 1959; [70] Stewart 1942; [71] Stoffle et al. 1989; [78] Train et al. 1941; [79] Van Valkenburgh 1976; [87] Zigmond 1981.

Rose Family (Rosaceae)

Woods' Rose

Rosa woodsii Lindl. var. *ultramontana* (S. Wats.) Jepson

Figures 64, 65

Owens Valley Paiute: *tsiava* [65]; *"te-ah-we-hah," "tea-yava"* (bush), *"te-ah-vow-yah"* (red berry) [49]
Southern Paiute: *ciampibɨ* [57]; *cɨ'impipi* (hips) [48]
Western Shoshone: *"see-avvie," "see-am-bip"* [78]; *ci'abi* [57]

Description and Habitat

Woods' rose is a many-branched, prickly shrub growing up to about 3 feet in height, with prominent pink flowers arranged around an urn-shaped floral cup [18, 57]. This cup later enlarges and encloses the seeds in a fleshy, reddish orange hip. Wild rose is not common in southern Nevada, being found locally in moist settings near springs or washes at higher elevations in the mountains [5]. Thickets can be found in moist settings in most of the large mountain ranges in the southern Great Basin, usually associated with pinyon pine, yellow pine, or fir [5].

Native Uses

Rose hips, an excellent source of vitamin C, were collected and eaten by most Native groups in the Great Basin [9, 49, 66, 87]. The Timbisha ate the

Figure 64. Woods' rose
(*Rosa woodsii* var. *ultra-montana*)

fruits and called them "*zay-beah-ah-ph*" [49]. Southern Paiute people also used the fruits [9]. The Owens Valley Paiute people only occasionally ate the seeds [65], but they did use the flower buds for food.

Wild rose was an important medicinal plant [78]. A tea made from the steeped leaves was widely esteemed both as a beverage and tonic. A tea made from roots or inner bark was used as a cure for colds or as a diuretic. Various parts of the plant were used to dress cuts, sores, wounds, burns, and swellings. The plant material was collected, saved, and applied dry or moistened as needed. Peeled stems were made into powder or shavings, placed in a wound, and covered with a bandage. The shavings alleviated swelling and pain and promoted healing. A Native consultant from Beatty reported that the seeds were useful for easing bowel disorders [78]. The plant is still used for medicinal purposes today [43].

The Southern Paiute and Owens Valley Paiute used wild rose branches to make arrow shafts, but these had to be greased when dry to prevent cracking [48, 55]. The Kawaiisu used unsplit wild rose stems as rims of twined baskets [87].

Figure 65. Woods' rose
(Rosa woodsii var. *ultra-montana)* fruits

Owens Valley people strung rose buds together to make necklaces [49], and Southern Paiute girls did the same with rose hips [48].

Sources: [5] Beatley 1976; [9] Bye 1972; [18] Cronquist et al. 1997; [48] Kelly 1964; [49] Kerr 1936; [55] V. Miller, pers. commun.; [57] Mozingo 1987; [65] Steward 1933; [66] Steward 1938; [78] Train et al. 1941; [87] Zigmond 1981.

Honeysuckle Family (Caprifoliaceae)

Desert Snowberry

Symphoricarpos longiflorus Gray

Figures 66, 67

Southern Paiute: *tampisudupi* [57]; *avagunimpi* [52]

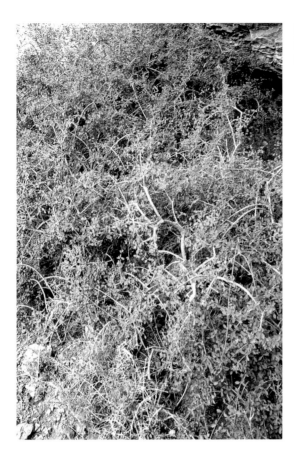

Figure 66. Desert snow-
berry *(Symphoricarpos longiflorus)*

Description and Habitat

Desert snowberry is a spreading to straggling shrub that grows to 1–4 feet
high. It has red to grayish branches, shreddy bark, and twigs that grow opposite each other [16, 41]. The small, round to oval leaves are also paired opposite one another. Its trumpet-shaped flowers are pink and measure about
0.50–0.75 inch long; flowers mature into round or oval waxy white berries
when ripe [57]. Desert snowberry is common in the foothills and mountains
of the region, especially at the base of cliffs, rock ledges, and along washes
[5], but it inhabits drier slopes as well [57]. It grows between 3800 and
7400 feet elevation in blackbrush, sagebrush, and pinyon-juniper communities [5].

Native Uses

A tea was made from the boiled plant to relieve indigestion [78]. People
smoked the leaves of some species of snowberry [62]. The shredding bark of
a related species, *S. oreophilus,* was used to make string, especially in the

Figure **67**. Desert snowberry *(Symphoricarpos
longiflorus)* flower

northern Great Basin [66]. Long shoots of the snowberry species *S. racemo-
sus* were used to make arrow shafts for taking birds [58]. These shafts are
light and have a thick pith, which could be hollowed out to make an arrow
of any desired weight. Snowberry shrubs were cut down in autumn so that
the following spring new shoots would grow straight and smooth, ready for
harvest by the next autumn. Berries of this plant may have been used for
food [43, 71].

Sources: [5] Beatley 1976; [16] Cronquist et al. 1984; [41] Hickman 1993; [43] Y.
Jake, pers. commun.; [52] Lawlor 1995; [57] Mozingo 1987; [58] Murphey 1959;
[62] Palmer 1878; [66] Steward 1938; [71] Stoffle et al. 1989; [78] Train et al.
1941.

Currant Family (Grossulariaceae)
Gooseberry
Ribes spp.

Figures 68–70

Owens Valley Paiute: *"boh-ho-crima"* [49]
Southern Paiute: *pogompi* (for *Ribes aureum*) [48]
Western Shoshone: *"dembogen,"* *"bogumbe"* [58]; *ohapogombi*
 (for *Ribes aureum*) [57]; *engapogombi* (for *Ribes cereum*) [57];
 mugubogombi (for *Ribes velutinum*) [57]

Description and Habitat

Gooseberry, or currant, is a rounded multibranched shrub reaching 6 feet or more in height, with clusters of leaves at the ends of short branches [18, 41, 57]. The round to wedge-shaped leaves are three to five lobed, with conspicuous light green veins. Clusters of small white flowers in spring give way to abundant juicy, red to black berries in summer. Several species of gooseberry grow in the southern Great Basin [5, 18], most often in meadows and forests at elevations above 6000 feet. These include the golden currant *(Ribes aureum)* and the wax currant *(Ribes cereum)* [5]. One species, the desert or plateau gooseberry *(Ribes velutinum)* [57] grows on dry volcanic mountain slopes associated with sagebrush and pinyon-juniper woodland at elevations above 5300 feet [5].

Figure 68. Golden currant *(Ribes aureum)* bush

Figure 69. Wax currant *(Ribes cereum)* flowers

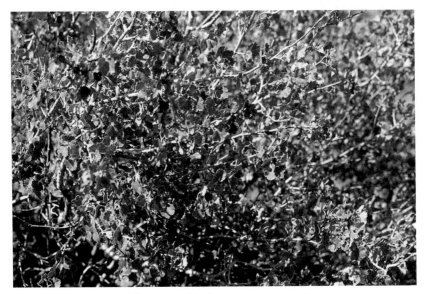

Figure 70. Wax currant *(Ribes cereum)* fruits

Native Uses

Gooseberries, including the desert gooseberry, were among several berries widely collected during the summer by Native groups in the Great Basin [49, 67]. The most important species to be collected were the golden and wax currants. The berries were usually cooked in a small amount of water.

LARGE SHRUBS AND WOODY VINES

Berries were eaten fresh in June and July or dried in the shade and stored [49, 65, 87]. Dried berries were soaked in water or boiled. Fresh berries were boiled with a little sugar to make jelly [87]. The Kaibab Southern Paiute ate fresh berries of the golden currant, and children ate the wax currant, but the latter were thought to cause headaches [48].

Some Western Shoshone groups used the inner bark of golden currant to cure sores [78]. The straight, hard stems were often used to make arrow or spear shafts [48, 66].

Sources: [5] Beatley 1976; [18] Cronquist et al. 1997; [41] Hickman 1993; [48] Kelly 1964; [49] Kerr 1936; [57] Mozingo 1987; [58] Murphey 1959; [65] Steward 1933; [67] Steward 1941; [78] Train et al. 1941; [87] Zigmond 1981.

Rose Family (Rosaceae)

Utah Serviceberry

Amelanchier utahensis Koehne

Figures 71–73

Southern Paiute: *tiabi, tiwampi, tiwabi* [29]; *toyaba, toyabe* [61]; *tiav* (the plant), *tiwampi* (berries) [48]
Western Shoshone: *düem* [66]; *tiampi* [29]; *ti'ampi* [57]

Figure 71. Serviceberry *(Amelanchier utahensis)*

Figure 72. Serviceberry
(Amelanchier utahensis)
flowers

Figure 73. Serviceberry *(Amelanchier utahensis)* fruits

LARGE SHRUBS AND WOODY VINES

Description and Habitat

Utah serviceberry is a large spreading shrub with ovate leaves that grows to 3–12 feet tall [18, 41]. The shrub bears a profusion of small white flowers in late spring and early summer, followed by small purplish fruits that persist in a dried state on the branches into fall [18]. Serviceberry grows in the larger mountains of southern Nevada, between about 5000 and 9000 feet elevation, associated with sagebrush, pinyon, juniper, yellow pine, and fir [5]. It inhabits open rocky slopes, washes, cliffs, and rock outcrops.

Native Uses

The small currantlike fruits of Utah serviceberry were collected and eaten by many peoples in the Great Basin and throughout western North America [11, 48, 61, 66, 87]. The Southern Paiute gathered the berries in the fall, dried them, and ground them to be eaten with water "like canned tomatoes" [48]. Some groups mixed dried fruits with dried meat to make pemmican, an important winter food. The seeds were also used "mashed and made into small cakes for drying and storing" [66]. Utah serviceberry also had medicinal value. An eyewash was made from the green inner bark boiled with sugar; this was used for snowblindness [78].

Serviceberry wood was highly prized for the construction of a variety of utilitarian objects. Branches were used for arrow shafts, cradleboard frames, basket rims, digging sticks, and bows [48, 66, 87], although some people thought serviceberry branches were too small for bows [67].

Sources: [5] Beatley 1976; [11] Chamberlin 1911; [18] Cronquist et al. 1997; [29] Fowler 1972; [41] Hickman 1993; [48] Kelly 1964; [49] Kerr 1936; [57] Mozingo 1987; [61] Palmer 1871; [66] Steward 1938; [67] Steward 1941; [87] Zigmond 1981.

Honeysuckle Family (Caprifoliaceae)

Blue Elderberry

Sambucus cerulea var. *cerulea* C. Presl.

Figures 74–76

Owens Valley Paiute: *pagubu'xia, sai'inoiya'a* [65]; *"sino-we-ah"* [49]; *"hubu"* [55]
Southern Paiute: *kunuk'wi* [48]; *"kon-vee"* [53]
Timbisha Shoshone: *"ko-no-weepaha," "kono-whee(p),"* *"kono-kee-per"* [49]

Figure 74. Blue elderberry *(Sambucus cerulea)*

Description and Habitat

Blue elderberry is a large, typically multitrunked spreading shrub or small tree, standing 6–25 feet tall and nearly as wide [16, 41]. The leaves are composed of five to nine smooth-surfaced leaflets that are green above, paler below, and finely toothed along the edges [16, 57]. In the spring, flat-topped or umbrella-like clusters of delicate white flowers form at the ends of branches [16]. The flowers turn to clusters of bluish black berries covered with a dense waxy powder, thus appearing blue [57]. Blue elderberry grows in moist places along streams or under shaded cliffs in pinyon-juniper woodlands and yellow pine or fir forests between 5600 and 9100 feet elevation [5].

Native Uses

Elderberries were one of the main berries to be gathered in midsummer. The berries were eaten fresh or boiled in pots with a small amount of water to make a jelly [48, 65, 87]. Spreading them on rocks to dry in the sun also preserved the berries. The dried fruits were then stored in skin bags, which were hung up for winter use [65]. Elderberry jam remains a favorite of Native people today [43, 53].

Other parts of the plant had medicinal value. Elderberry flowers and leaves were boiled, and a person would lean over the steaming liquid and breathe in the vapors to relieve colds and headaches [87]. A tea made of flowers was drunk to relieve fever or measles. To cure blood poisoning, the afflicted limb was soaked in a hot liquid made by boiling elderberry leaves.

LARGE SHRUBS AND WOODY VINES

Figure 75. Blue elder-
berry *(Sambucus cerulea)*
flowers

Figure 76. Blue elderberry *(Sambucus cerulea)* fruits

Native doctors made six-hole flutes or whistles by removing the soft pith from the center of elderberry branches and used these flutes in curing rites [65, 87]. Hollowed-out branch sections were also fashioned into holders for plugs of tobacco or a tobacco-lime mixture. The stems were also used in making baskets and cradleboards [43]. Arrow and dart shafts made from elderberry canes have been found in archaeological sites in the eastern Mojave Desert [19].

Sources: [5] Beatley 1976; [16] Cronquist et al. 1984; [19] Davis et al. 1981; [41] Hickman 1993; [43] Y. Jake, pers. commun.; [48] Kelly 1964; [49] Kerr 1936; [53] C. Lynch, pers. commun.; [55] V. Miller, pers. commun.; [57] Mozingo 1987; [65] Steward 1933; [67] Steward 1941; [87] Zigmond 1981.

CHAPTER THREE

Small Shrubs and Subshrubs

Goosefoot Family (Chenopodiaceae)

Mojave Seablite

Suaeda moquinii (Torr.) Greene

Figure 77

Owens Valley Paiute: *"pe-hah-da-da"* [49]
Southern Paiute: *"ahrr," "aah-ap-weep," "sah-ap-weep"* [9]; *adimpi* [57]
Western Shoshone: *attem* [78]; *atimpi* [57]

Description and Habitat

Mojave seablite (also known as seepweed) is a sooty-looking, greenish gray perennial subshrub that grows to 1–2 feet high [42, 57]. Its thin shiny yellowish brown branches rise from a woody base [41]. These spreading branches are sparsely covered with flat narrow leaves that are about 1 inch long, giving an overall scraggly appearance [57]. The flowers are small, greenish, and inconspicuous. The plant is common in saline or alkaline

Figure 77. Mojave seablite *(Suaeda moquinii)*

environments, including playa margins, alkali flats (with fourwing saltbush and creosote bush), and sandy flats or dunes (with mesquite) [5, 57]. Mojave seablite can thrive in salty and alkali soils where moisture is near the surface [5].

Native Uses

Seablite seeds were sometimes eaten [9], and the green plant was eaten raw [49]. Stems and leaves were mashed and used as a poultice for cuts and sores [71] and rubbed on chicken pox sores to dry them and alleviate the pain [78]. A tea made from the plant eased bladder and kidney troubles [78]. A black ink or dye can be made from the herbage [42].

Sources: [5] Beatley 1976; [9] Bye 1972; [41] Hickman 1993; [42] Jaeger 1941; [49] Kerr 1936; [57] Mozingo 1987; [71] Stoffle et al. 1989; [72] Stoffle et al. 1990; [78] Train et al. 1941.

Mallow Family (Malvaceae)

Desert Globe Mallow

Sphaeralcea ambigua Gray

Figures 78, 79

Owens Valley Paiute: *"weedogova"* [78]; *"muha"* [55, 58]
Southern Paiute: *gubanap* [66]; *kuikumpɨ* [48]; *"kuku-pa-ni-ve"* [53]; *"koopena"* [58]
Timbisha Shoshone: *"we-tho-ko"* [49]; *gwidegomb:* [66]
Western Shoshone: *"wee-doh-comb," "quoin-oh-combee," "wee-dah-gom," "quoya-no-comb," "see-quoy no-ko"* [78]

Description and Habitat

Desert globe mallow is a perennial subshrub that grows to 1–3 feet tall and about as broad, and it is often woody near the base [41, 42]. The plant's green lobed leaves, resembling those of a geranium, are covered with fine star-shaped hairs [41]. Flowers are apricot to reddish orange and up to 1.5 inches wide. In flower, desert globe mallow is conspicuous on roadsides and disturbed areas, and it grows in a wide variety of habitats and plant communities in the southern Great Basin below about 7000 feet elevation [5].

Native Uses

Death Valley and Owens Valley people boiled the mallow plant to make a thick syrup, which was then mixed with potter's clay and used to coat drying

Figure 78. Desert globe mallow *(Sphaeralcea ambigua)*

Figure 79. Foliage and flowers of desert globe mallow *(Sphaeralcea ambigua)*

pots [49, 65, 66]. Whether this additive strengthened the pot, prevented brittleness, or affected the firing is not certain. People at Ash Meadows and in the Lida area apparently did not practice this technique [66].

A drink made from boiled mallow roots was used to treat various maladies. The boiled leaves yielded a solution used as an eyewash [78].

Seeds were cooked and ground for food [48, 49], and the fruits were apparently eaten as well [71].

Sources: [5] Beatley 1976; [41] Hickman 1993; [42] Jaeger 1941; [48] Kelly 1964; [49] Kerr 1936; [55] V. Miller, pers. commun.; [58] Murphey 1959; [65] Steward 1933; [66] Steward 1938; [71] Stoffle et al. 1989; [78] Train et al. 1941.

Sunflower Family (Asteraceae)

Brittlebush

Encelia farinosa Gray ex Torr.

Figure 80

Southern Paiute: *suopiv* [71]

Description and Habitat

Brittlebush is a hemispherical shrub that grows up to 4 feet high and as broad across [14]. It bears abundant silvery grayish green leaves, which turn white and die back in the hot dry summer months [42]. In spring, the shrub is covered with chrome yellow, daisylike flowers rising above the leaves. Brittlebush is common in washes and along lower canyon walls of limestone or calcareous ridges; it grows in association with creosote bush, spiny hopsage, wolfberry, and blackbrush communities [5].

Figure 80. Brittlebush
(Encelia farinosa)

SMALL SHRUBS AND SUBSHRUBS

Brittlebush stems were used in making baskets [71]. Historically, the leaves and flowers were boiled and the liquid used as a wash for the relief of rheumatism [42] or to help heal cuts and bruises on horses [87].

Sources: [5] Beatley 1976; [14] Cronquist 1994; [42] Jaeger 1941; [71] Stoffle et al. 1989; [87] Zigmond 1981.

Mustard Family (Brassicaceae)

Desert Prince's Plume
Stanleya pinnata (Pursh) Britt.

Figure 81

Owens Valley Paiute: *yuhuara* [71]; *"ter-water," "we-water"* [49]
Southern Paiute: *tumar* [71]; *tiˀmadɨ* [29]; *timarɨ* [48]; *"tumani"* [53]
Western Shoshone: *tuwarra, tuhuara* [71]; *"woy-boh-numb"* [78]

Description and Habitat

Desert prince's plume is a perennial subshrub with a woody base and leafy stems that reach 2–3 feet [41]. The leaves are dark green and lanceolate in overall shape, with edges that may be smooth, toothed, or deeply lobed. Prominent flowering stalks rise another 2–3 feet above the foliage [41, 42]. In late spring and early summer, these stalks support plumes of bright yellow flowers. Desert prince's plume is one of the earliest small shrubs to leaf out in the spring. It prefers sandy or gravelly soils near washes or alluvial fans, mainly in desert shrub communities, and is often found in areas of ground disturbance [5]. The plant thrives in selenium-rich soils and is known to take up large quantities of this element [42]. The high selenium content may poison animals grazing on the leaves.

Native Uses

Leaves of desert prince's plume were an important source of dietary greens in the spring. Plants were intensively managed through certain methods of harvesting and pruning to ensure a stable and reliable supply in succeeding years [33, 71]. The young leaves and stems were usually boiled, squeezed out in cold water to remove bitterness, and then boiled and washed two to four times [48]; one might get sick otherwise [42]. The greens are similar to spinach in nutritive value, but have much higher levels of the potentially toxic element selenium. Boiling removes much of the bitter astringency and

Figure 81. Desert prince's plume (Stanleya pinnata)

selenium that the leaves naturally contain. Desert prince's plume is one of several plants growing in the Mojave Desert that was processed in this way to remove bitterness from the leaves [12]. The plant is still sought out today, and the leaves are stored in the freezer and used throughout the year [43]. Today the boiled leaves are often fried with grease or bacon, like collard greens [43, 53]. Desert prince's plume root also was valued as medicine, mainly for external treatment of injuries and pain [78].

Sources: [5] Beatley 1976; [12] Coville 1892; [29] Fowler 1972; [33] Fowler 1996; [41] Hickman 1993; [42] Jaeger 1941; [43] Y. Jake, pers. commun.; [48] Kelly 1964; [49] Kerr 1936; [53] C. Lynch, pers. commun.; [71] Stoffle et al. 1989; [78] Train et al. 1941.

SMALL SHRUBS AND SUBSHRUBS

Rue Family (Rutaceae)

Turpentine Broom

Thamnosma montana Torr. & Frém.

Figure 82

Owens Valley Paiute: *"mogo-du-heupie"* [49]
Southern Paiute: *mugru'upi* [71]; *"moo-ga-hu-pe"* [53]; *"mogorup"* [58];
mua-buip^i [47]
Timbisha Shoshone: *"mogundo," "mogodoo," "mocodope"* [49]
Western Shoshone: *"mo-gun-du," "moh-goon-du-oop"* [78];
"ma-good-te-hoo" [58]

Description and Habitat

Turpentine broom is a branching, broomlike, yellowish green shrub that
grows to 1–3 feet high. Its stems and tiny leaves are covered with glands.
Often the gland-dotted stems are without leaves. The bluish purple, 0.5-inch
flowers blossom in the spring. These become pea-sized, gland-dotted, two-
lobed, saclike fruits that yield an irritating but citruslike oil [42]. Turpentine
broom grows in washes and on slopes and disturbed soils of bajadas with
creosote bush, wolfberry, blackbrush, sagebrush, and saltbush below 5000
feet elevation [5].

Native Uses

This low bush has medicinal and mind-altering properties. The boiled stems
and leaves of turpentine broom made a tea used as a tonic and to treat colds,

Figure 82. Turpentine broom *(Thamnosma montana)*

chest pains, smallpox, and female complaints [78]. It is said that the tea makes a person "crazy like coyotes" for a while [42, 87], but one could find lost objects while in that state. The Southern Paiute made use of the plant as a tea to treat internal disorders or as a laxative [47, 48]. The plant was made into a poultice for sores [49], and open wounds healed quickly when a powder of the plant [42, 87] or crushed leaves [47] was applied. The stems were dried, ground, and mixed with commercial tobacco to be smoked as a cure for colds [78] or as a tobacco substitute [49]. The Timbisha smoked the plant or chewed the bark. The plant was also burned on a hot rock and the smoke inhaled by several people, which was said to induce sleep [49]. The Southern Paiute used turpentine broom to dye basket willows yellow [58], and the sharp stem tips were used to pierce ears [71].

The Kawaiisu placed a powder made of turpentine broom in deer tracks to help the hunt. The smelly powder also kept snakes away and generally caused trouble for enemies [87]. The Western Shoshone burned this plant, mixed with juniper and antelope bush *(Purshia tridentata)*, to ward off evil spirits [58]. The plant should not be carried on horseback, however, "because it will cause the horse to swell up" [58].

Sources: [5] Beatley 1976; [42] Jaeger 1941; [48] Kelly 1964; [49] Kerr 1936; [53] C. Lynch, pers. commun.; [58] Murphey 1959; [71] Stoffle et al. 1989; [78] Train et al. 1941; [87] Zigmond 1981.

Sunflower Family (Asteraceae)

Brownplume Wirelettuce
Stephanomeria pauciflora (Torr.) A. Nels.

Figures 83, 84

Southern Paiute: *saŋakovɨ* [48]

Description and Habitat

Wirelettuce (sometimes called skeletonweed) is a subshrub or perennial herb that grows up to 2 feet high on erect, wiry branching stems from a woody base [14, 41]. When broken, the stems exude a thick milky sap. The sparse leaves are long and thin. Small elongated flower heads are terminal on the branchlets, with conspicuous pink to reddish petal-like ray flowers [14, 42]. Wirelettuce is widely distributed throughout southern Nevada in disturbed or sandy soils in open areas. It can often be seen growing along roadsides, as a pale green, hemispheric shrub. Wirelettuce is found in association with creosote bush, saltbush, winterfat, wolfberry, burrobush, big sagebrush, pinyon, and juniper between 3000 and 6500 feet elevation [5].

Figure 83. Brownplume wirelettuce *(Stephanomeria pauciflora)*

Figure 84. Leave and feathery fruits (achenes) of brownplume wire-lettuce *(Stephanomeria pauciflora)*

SMALL SHRUBS AND SUBSHRUBS

Native Uses

Different species of wirelettuce were used for a variety of purposes, mostly medicinal. A rubbery gummy extract was scraped off the stems and roots and chewed [65, 71, 78, 87]. According to some consultants, the plant is still in use for this purpose today [71]. A cottony fuzz found at the base of thorn skeletonweed *(Stephanomeria spinosa)* was collected and placed on sores to promote healing [78]. The boiled roots were used as an eyewash and for other medicinal purposes [78]. A related plant, narrowleaved wirelettuce *(Stephanomeria tenuifolia)*, was boiled to make a tea for treatment of venereal disease [78].

Sources: [5] Beatley 1976; [14] Cronquist 1994; [41] Hickman 1993; [42] Jaeger 1941; [48] Kelly 1964; [65] Steward 1933; [71] Stoffle et al. 1989; [78] Train et al. 1941; [87] Zigmond 1981.

Sunflower Family (Asteraceae)

Threadleaf Snakeweed
Gutierrezia microcephala (DC.) Gray

Broom Snakeweed
Gutierrezia sarothrae (Pursh) Britt. & Rusby

Figure 85

Western Shoshone: *tavishepi* [71]

Description and Habitat

Snakeweed, a woody-based perennial subshrub, grows in a rounded clump 8–24 inches high [16, 57]. In late summer or fall, it is topped with many small yellow flowers. Snakeweed gets its name because it is said that a poultice made from ground, boiled leaves reduces swelling inflicted by snakebite in sheep [42]. Snakeweed is widely distributed and is common to abundant in many plant communities. It grows on slopes and ridges, in washes, and on rock outcrops, particularly where soils are derived from calcareous rock. Snakeweed is commonly associated with saltbush, blackbrush, sagebrush, and pinyon-juniper communities; it is less commonly associated with creosote bush, saltbush-winterfat, and spiny hopsage–wolfberry communities [5].

Native Uses

A tea was made from snakeweed leaves to cure colds, and a hot poultice of the leaves was applied to sprains or aches [71, 78]. According to one consultant,

Figure 85. Snakeweed *(Gutierrezia sarothrae)*

this bush can be scary when you walk by it because it makes the sound of a rattlesnake buzzing [56].

Sources: [5] Beatley 1976; [14] Cronquist 1994; [42] Jaeger 1941; [56] B. Moose, pers. commun.; [57] Mozingo 1987; [71] Stoffle et al. 1989; [78] Train et al. 1941.

Goosefoot Family (Chenopodiaceae)

Winterfat

Krascheninnikovia lanata (Pursh) A.D.J. Meeuse & Smit

Figure 86

Western Shoshone: *"shee-shub," "tuh-veep"* [78]; *"sissop"* [58]

Description and Habitat

Winterfat is a low-growing shrub that reaches 1–2 feet in height and is densely covered with wooly white hairs [42]. The upper silvery white twigs become pale and rust colored with age. Leaves are oblong and flat with in-rolled edges [41]. The flowers are borne in small dense clusters where leaf and stem intersect. Winterfat retains its foliage and fruit throughout the winter, making it an important forage plant for deer and livestock [57]. It is

Figure 86. Winterfat *(Krascheninnikovia lanata)*

common from the Mojave Desert of California through Nevada and Idaho in numerous Great Basin plant communities [5, 42].

Native Uses

A hot solution of winterfat was used to rid the head of lice. Some consultants thought it prevented hair from falling out and restored hair growth as baldness set in [78]. Tea made from the leaves was used as a general beverage and a shampoo [58]. The Timbisha also drank the tea for respiratory ailments [25].

Sources: [5] Beatley 1976; [25] P. Esteves, pers. commun.; [41] Hickman 1993; [42] Jaeger 1941; [57] Mozingo 1987; [58] Murphey 1959; [78] Train et al. 1941.

Ratany Family (Krameriaceae)

Littleleaf Ratany
Krameria erecta Willd. ex J. A. Schultes

Figures 87, 88

Southern Paiute: *nagavaronump* [71]; *"nagavarodam"* [53]; *"nah-kah-vah dah-tohnub"* [78]; *naka' borinanimp* [48]; *"pahaab"* [58]
Western Shoshone: *"nah-gee-too-nah-nib"* [78]

SMALL SHRUBS AND SUBSHRUBS

Figure 87. Littleleaf ratany *(Krameria erecta)*

Figure 88. Littleleaf ratany *(Krameria erecta)* foliage and fruits

Description and Habitat

Littleleaf ratany (also known as purple heather) is a low shrub, usually less than 2 feet high, but it sprawls up to 4 feet in diameter [18, 42]. New leaves are covered with soft hair that becomes coarser with age. It has rigid branches and small but strikingly beautiful reddish purple flowers, which are followed by small, globose, green fruits covered with stiff red hairs [18]. Littleleaf ratany usually grows with Fremont's dalea in creosote bush and saltbush communities on bajadas below limestone mountain ranges at 2300–4200 feet elevation [5].

Native Uses

The tiny seeds of littleleaf ratany were collected as food, and the root was used as a dye [53, 71]. The root was also boiled to make a wash for swellings or dried to make a powder applied to sores [78]. The plant was also used as an emetic [48].

Sources: [5] Beatley 1976; [18] Cronquist et al. 1997; [42] Jaeger 1941; [48] Kelly 1964; [53] C. Lynch, pers. commun.; [58] Murphey 1959; [71] Stoffle et al. 1989; [78] Train et al. 1941.

Mint Family (Lamiaceae)

Purple Sage
Salvia dorrii (Kellogg) Abrams

Figure 89

Owens Valley Paiute: *"see-goo-we-up"* [55]
Southern Paiute: *nungwukoap, kwatamanum* [71]; *siguwiipi* [48]; *siʔapi* [50]; *"se-gwe-yan"* [53]; *"see-goo-we-up"* [78]
Western Shoshone: *kaibasi'tum* [66]; *"kahn-gwanna," "suh-goo-wee-up," "toya-abba-hobe," "toay-tim-ba-zip"* [78]

Description and Habitat

Purple sage is a round-topped shrub that grows up to 3 feet tall with dense branches [16, 41, 57]. The branches are ridged, spine-tipped, and covered with silvery green, hairy, rounded leaves, each of which measure 0.5–1.0 inch long. The shrub is covered with two-lipped, deep purple flowers in the spring. Purple sage grows on volcanic and limestone substrates on dry slopes and washes. It is found in sagebrush, pinyon-juniper, creosote bush–burrobush, and blackbrush communities between 3200 and 7500 feet elevation [5].

Native Uses

The aromatic leaves of purple sage are a valued medicine. A tea boiled from the leaves is useful for stomach troubles, colds, and other ailments [66, 78, 87]. Hot tea was given to children with sore throats. Dried leaves were smoked for medicinal purposes, a practice that continues today [71]. The plant had external uses as well. The tops of the plant were boiled, and the solution was applied as an external wash for swollen leg veins [78]. Sores were washed

Figure 89. Purple sage *(Salvia dorrii)*

with a tea made of the leaves or with water containing dried pulverized leaves [48]. The Kawaiisu used a similar wash to help relieve headaches [87].

The Kawaiisu also threw the plant into the campfire or left some in a frying pan over the fire at night, making smoke to keep ghosts away [87]. The Chemehuevi Southern Paiute preferred sage branches as a thatching material in the construction of brush houses [50]. Purple sage currently plays an important role in the Native American Church, where it is used in a smoke mixture for prayers and its branches are used as a fan [43].

Sources: [5] Beatley 1976; [16] Cronquist et al. 1984; [41] Hickman 1993; [43] Y. Jake, pers. commun.; [48] Kelly 1964; [50] Laird 1976; [53] C. Lynch, pers. commun.; [55] V. Miller, pers. commun.; [57] Mozingo 1987; [66] Steward 1938; [71] Stoffle et al. 1989; [78] Train et al. 1941; [87] Zigmond 1981.

Sunflower Family (Asteraceae)

Mountain Sagewort
Artemisia ludoviciana Nutt. ssp. *incompta* (Nutt.) Keck

Figure 90

Southern Paiute: *pa 'sangwav* [71]; *saŋwabt* [29]; *"poss-paws,"* *"salm-ap-weep," "pas"* [9]
Western Shoshone: *"pawots"* [58]

Figure 90. Mountain sagewort *(Artemisia ludoviciana* ssp. *incompta)*

Description and Habitat

Mountain sagewort is a perennial herb with herbaceous stems that bear white hairs [14, 41]. Its fragrant leaves are divided into segments and are sparsely hairy. This plant is widely distributed in middle elevations (4100–7600 feet) in southern Nevada [5]. It is commonly found in sandy or rocky soils, sometimes on dry slopes associated with shadscale, blackbrush, and sagebrush, but more typically in mesic habitats such as cliff bases, in washes, and around boulders [5].

Native Uses

Leaves of this highly valued plant were boiled to make a medicinal tea. The tea aided in childbirth; remedied headaches, colds, and worms; and was a stimulant. The leaves of mountain sagewort were used to plug nosebleeds. Mountain sagewort is still used today by Native people in southern and central Nevada [71].

The closely related wormwood *(Artemisia dracunculus)* was boiled and placed as a hot poultice for sprains, swellings, sore throats, swollen neck glands, and rheumatism. A tea from this plant was drunk or used as a wash following childbirth, to relieve external stings, or to treat venereal disease [78].

The Southern Paiute used to grind up a mixture of the seeds of mountain sagewort and wormwood (called *pasi*) to make a strong-flavored gruel [9, 43, 48].

Sources: [5] Beatley 1976; [9] Bye 1972; [14] Cronquist 1994; [29] Fowler 1972; [41] Hickman 1993; [43] Y. Jake, pers. commun.; [48] Kelly 1964; [58] Murphey 1959; [71] Stoffle et al. 1989; [78] Train et al. 1941.

CHAPTER FOUR

Yuccas and Agaves

Lily Family (Liliaceae)

Mojave Yucca
Yucca schidigera Roezl ex Ortgies

Figures 91, 92

Southern Paiute: *tachumb, u'vimp* [53, 71]; *chumba* [53]; *'uuvimpɨ* [50]; *tcɨmpi* (fruits) [50]; *uwimpi* [32]; *uwimpi, uuvimpi, tatsiimpi* (whole plant) [46, 52]

Description and Habitat

Mojave yucca (also known as Spanish dagger or Spanish bayonet [42]), reaches 3–15 feet in height; trough-shaped yellowish green leaves grow up to 3 feet long and cover the main trunk and occasional side branches [7, 42]. Older leaves tend to fray at the margins, revealing strong, coarse fibers [7]. A dense flowering spike appears in spring with a prominent cluster of creamy

Figure 91. Mojave yucca *(Yucca schidigera)*

Figure 92. Mojave yucca
(*Yucca schidigera*) flowers

white flowers, sometimes tinged with lavender [42]. These are followed in early summer by a cluster of fleshy green fruits with a thick outer covering; each fruit measures about 2–3 inches long and about half as wide [7]. Mojave yucca inhabits rocky or gravelly slopes below about 7000 feet elevation [41] throughout much of the eastern and central Mojave Desert [42]. It is the most common yucca found in the interior Mojave Desert [42] and is often associated with creosote bush–burrobush or saltbush communities [5].

Native Uses

This is one of several yuccas used extensively for food by Mojave Desert peoples, part of what anthropologist Catherine Fowler calls the "yucca complex" of Mojave Desert foods [32]. The small fruits of the Mojave yucca were sometimes roasted and eaten [32], although this yucca was apparently not used as much as other species. The Owens Valley Paiute ate the sweet-tasting flowers and called them *ma-huve-gar* [49]. The strong leaf fibers were used for making baskets or sandals [46, 50]. The pithy insides of Mojave yucca leaves were used as a soap and shampoo [53, 55, 71]. Leaves were also tied together to make a slow match for carrying fire [48]. Food and fibers were stored for long-term use [71].

Sources: [7] Benson and Darrow 1981; [32] Fowler 1995; [41] Hickman 1993; [42] Jaeger 1941; [46] Kelly 1932–1934; [48] Kelly 1964; [49] Kerr 1936; [50] Laird 1976; [52] Lawlor 1995; [53] C. Lynch, pers. commun.; [55] V. Miller, pers. commun.; [71] Stoffle et al. 1989.

Lily Family (Liliaceae)

Banana Yucca
Yucca baccata Torr.

Figures 93, 94

Southern Paiute: *u'wivi* [71]; *kaayuvimpi̵, kaiuwimpi* [46, 52]; *tci̵mpi* (fruits) [50]; *uusi* [32, 48]; *us, usö, tcömaupö* [70]; *"ochive," "osh"* [53]; *"datil"* (from Spanish), *"ooss"* [58] Timbisha Shoshone: *"mow-pava"* [49]

Description and Habitat

The banana yucca is distinguished by its low, stemless appearance (the stems are actually underground) [15]; the long bluish gray leaves arranged in a spiky mound [42]; and the long, smooth, green fruit pods ripening in

Figure 93. Banana yucca *(Yucca baccata)*

Figure 94. Banana yucca
(Yucca baccata) fruits

summer on the short-stalked central flowering spike [15]. Banana yucca is found on upper bajadas and slopes of limestone mountains on the margins of the eastern Mojave Desert. The plant grows in association with other yuccas, blackbrush or sagebrush scrub, and pinyon-juniper woodlands at 4500–7000 feet elevation [5].

Native Uses

Several different kinds of yuccas were important food plants for Mojave Desert peoples, and banana yucca was one of the main elements of this "yucca complex" of Mojave Desert foods [32]. The fleshy fruits of the banana yucca were gathered in the fall. They were cut into strips, the seeds were removed, and the flesh was dried for storage. The dried fruit was sweet and could be eaten like dried apples [43] or ground into a flour and made into cakes or mush. The Timbisha Shoshone may have cooked the tender stalk for food, according to Mark Kerr [49], but the common name Kerr used, Spanish bayonet, usually refers to *Yucca schidigera*.

YUCCAS AND AGAVES

The leaves were a source of strong, coarse fibers used in the construction of sandals, baskets, and other articles [9, 42, 55, 71]. Three dry leaves were tied together with fiber to make a slow match for carrying fire [46, 52]. The fibers and roots were used to make soap [9, 55] for cleaning a person or baskets because the soap did not dry out the basket or leave an oily residue [43]. Some groups used banana yucca soap in ceremonial wedding hair-washings [42]. According to Stoffle et al. [71], banana yucca is still used today for this purpose.

Sources: [5] Beatley 1976; [9] Bye 1972; [15] Cronquist et al. 1977; [32] Fowler 1995; [42] Jaeger 1941; [43] Y. Jake, pers commun.; [46] Kelly 1932–1934; [48] Kelly 1964; [49] Kerr 1936; [52] Lawlor 1995; [53] C. Lynch, pers. commun.; [55] V. Miller, pers. commun.; [58] Murphey 1959; [70] Stewart 1942; [71] Stoffle et al. 1989; [87] Zigmond 1981.

Lily Family (Liliaceae)

Joshua Tree
Yucca brevifolia Engelm.

Figures 97, 98

Owens Valley Paiute: *"ma-houve-gar"* (flowers), *"ma-puh-hee"* (fruits), *"pean"* [49]; *"pe-o ne"* (plant), *"ma-hou-ve-ga"* (flower) [56]
Southern Paiute: *tsoadimpi* [32]; *tsoarömpⁱ* [70]; *sovarampⁱ* (plant), *tcⁱmpi* (fruit) [50]
Timbisha Shoshone: *muupi* [32]; *"pah-key"* (flowers), *"pah-key-tava"* (fruits), *"oomp"* [49]
Western Shoshone: *umpu* [71]

Description and Habitat

For many, the Joshua tree is an emblem of the Mojave Desert [7]. Its stubby, twisted branches covered with spiky yellowish green leaves seem distinctively suited to the austere surroundings. Individual trees typically reach 15–30 feet high with a spread of 10–20 feet on a thick fibrous trunk [7, 34]. Large clusters of greenish white flowers appear on the ends of branches in the spring, followed by green, globose fruit pods that ripen in early summer [15].

The Joshua tree inhabits the outer edges of the Mojave Desert and grows on slopes of some of the higher mountain ranges, but is not common in the warmer and drier interior desert [7, 15, 42]. Joshua trees grow singly or in clusters on gravelly alluvial plains and ridges, generally at the upper limit of creosote bush scrub and lower limit of sagebrush and blackbrush, at 3500–7000 feet elevation [5, 15]. Common associates include

Figure 95. Joshua trees
(Yucca brevifolia) with
fruits

saltbush, wolfberry, spiny hopsage, *Ephedra,* blackbrush, and other typical
Mojave Desert shrubs [5].

Native Uses

Fruits of the Joshua tree were eaten boiled or pit-roasted like agave hearts;
they were cut in half, placed on top of dirt-covered coals in a pit, then sealed
over with dirt and steamed for a couple of days [71, 87]. According to anthropologist Catherine Fowler [32], some groups used these fruits for food
(e.g., the Timbisha Shoshone of Death Valley), whereas others did not (e.g.,
the Southern Paiute). The Death Valley Timbisha also ate the young flowering branch tips, twisting them off the ends of the branches and pit-roasting
them [12]. After cooking, the branch tips were "eaten much like an artichoke" [32, 49]. Mark Kerr [49] reported that the flowers were called *"pah-
key,"* the fruits were *"pah-key-tava,"* and cooked tender top spires of branches
were *go-tar-we.* Among the Owens Valley Paiute, the flowers *("ma-houve-
gar")* and fruits *("ma-puh-hee")* were both eaten, according to Kerr [49].
The Southern Paiute may have eaten the seeds raw and as a mush [9].

   Fibers from the leaves were used to make sandals [71]. Roots were used

YUCCAS AND AGAVES

Figure 96. Joshua tree *(Yucca brevifolia)* flower cluster

for red or brown design elements in basketry [9, 49, 87]. According to Stoffle et al. [71], young Joshua tree plants were traditionally transplanted to other areas to increase availability.

Sources: [5] Beatley 1976; [7] Benson and Darrow 1981; [9] Bye 1972; [12] Coville 1892; [15] Cronquist et al. 1977; [32] Fowler 1995; [34] Fowler and Fowler 1971; [42] Jaeger 1941; [49] Kerr 1936; [50] Laird 1976; [56] B. Moose, pers. commun.; [70] Stewart 1942; [71] Stoffle et al. 1989; [87] Zigmond 1981.

Agave Family (Agavaceae)
Utah Agave
Agave utahensis Engelm.

Figures 95, 96

Southern Paiute: *yant, yanti, nanti* [22, 32]; *nantapɨ* [50]; *yĕnt* [70]; *nant, yant* [46, 52]; *"yan-da"* [53]

Description and Habitat

Utah agave is recognized by a basal rosette of leaves that measures about 2 feet in diameter, which is composed of thick bluish leaves with marginal

Figure 97. Utah agave
(*Agave utahensis*)

teeth or spines, and an improbably tall thin flowering stalk that may exceed 7 feet in height [7, 17]. It tends to grow on limestone ridges between about 3000 and 7500 feet elevation, usually in association with Joshua trees and shadscale scrub but also growing amid pinyon and juniper woodlands [5, 7]. Utah agave grows in canyons on limestone mountains such as the Spring and Sheep Ranges [5]. Its distribution is the most northerly of any *Agave* species [7, 17], although it may not be the most cold-hardy; it appears to prefer the warmer lowland areas in the Mojave Desert [7]. Other species, including *Agave deserti* and *Agave parryi*, are common in the mountains of the Mojave and Sonoran Deserts [5, 7, 42].

Native Uses

Several species of agave were important food sources for Native peoples in the southern Great Basin and the warmer deserts to the south [32]. Agaves were available year-round, but people collected them in late winter or early spring, when other foods were scarce. At that time, just as the agave's basal rosette was full of stored sugars and was about to send up its flowering stalk, Southern Paiute and Chemehuevi collectors would gather in large groups to collect the agave hearts [48]. Collectors severed the rosettes from their roots with a digging stick, cut off the leaves with a specially made mescal knife, and carried the resulting fleshy hearts in a large burden basket to a central processing area for pit-roasting.

Women dug a pit 3 feet deep and 8–10 feet in diameter [48]. Stones were

Figure 98. Utah agave *(Agave utahensis)* basal rosette of leaves

laid in the bottom, a large fire was kindled on top, and the fire burned down to an even bed of hot coals. Women dumped their individual collections of agave hearts into the communal pit. Then the pit was covered with grass, juniper bark, and earth. The many hearts were baked together for one to two days, a time of much singing, dancing, gambling, and merry-making [73]. When the pit was opened, the cooked hearts were dark, soft, and sweet, tasting like molasses. People ate them fresh from the pit, or the hearts were cooled and formed into flat cakes for drying and storing [50]. These cakes (called *pikyovi* or *nantapikyovi* by the Chemehuevi) could be several feet in circumference and were very tough [50]. Dried cakes were often used as travel food [9]. One early explorer, Frederick Dellenbaugh, found the dried sheets to be a "powerful laxative. I could not eat much of it on that account" [45, 52].

Sometimes the leaves were roasted while still attached to the hearts, and they would be pulled off one by one and eaten "like a giant artichoke, the tough and stringy parts being discarded" [50]. According to Isabel Kelly, the leaves tasted "like burned sugar" [48]. In historic times, agave fibers were sometimes used as gun wads [9].

Sources: [5] Beatley 1976; [7] Benson and Darrow 1981; [9] Bye 1972; [15] Cronquist et al. 1977; [22] Ebeling 1986; [32] Fowler 1995; [42] Jaeger 1941; [43] Y. Jake, pers commun.; [45] Jones 1948; [46] Kelly 1932–1934; [48] Kelly 1964; [49] Kerr 1936; [50] Laird 1976; [52] Lawlor 1995; [53] C. Lynch, pers. commun.; [70] Stewart 1942; [73] Stuart 1945.

CHAPTER FIVE

Cacti

Cactus Family (Cactaceae)

Golden Cholla

Opuntia echinocarpa Engelm. & Bigelow

Figures 99, 100

Southern Paiute: *hintcungʷaramp* [50]
Western Shoshone: *wiatumbu* [71]

Description and Habitat

Golden cholla (also called silver or staghorn cholla) is a shrubby cactus that grows up to about 3–4 feet in height, with many short, spreading branches [41]. The branches are covered with sharp, straw-colored spines that are often more than 1 inch long, each one covered with a papery sheath [42]. If someone accidentally connects with one of these nasty spines, bits of the papery sheath can easily come off and lodge in the wound. It is said that the spines taste like witch hazel when wet [42]. The flower is a delicate lime green. The yellowish red fruit of the golden cholla is dry and spiny, with an odor of rancid butter [41]. Golden cholla is widely distributed throughout the region in creosote bush, saltbush, burrobush–wolfberry, blackbrush, and sagebrush communities below 5800 feet elevation [5].

Native Uses

The long sharp spines of the golden cholla were used as needles and awls for sewing and basketmaking [71]. The Owens Valley Paiute called the spines *winivep* [65]. Although the Kawaiisu name for this plant *(wiyaribi)* is derived from their name for awl *(waya),* the Kawaiisu used a different cactus (the cottontop or clustered barrel cactus, *Echinocactus polycephalus*) to make basketry awls [87]. Among the Southern Paiute cholla spines were used to pierce earlobes [43].

Pulp from the thick, succulent stems of the golden cholla was scraped out and used as a wet dressing for cuts and wounds to deaden pain and promote healing. The fine furze surrounding the spines was rubbed into warts or

Figure 99. Golden cholla
(Opuntia echinocarpa)

Figure 100. Golden cholla *(Opuntia echinocarpa)* flower

moles to remove them [78]. The Chemehuevi Southern Paiute gathered new branches just budding out (called *manavi*, their word for thorn) and cooked and ate them; the cooked buds had the consistency of jelly [50].

Sources: [5] Beatley 1976; [41] Hickman 1993; [42] Jaeger 1941; [43] Y. Jake, pers. commun.; [50] Laird 1976; [65] Steward 1933; [71] Stoffle et al. 1989; [78] Train et al. 1941; [87] Zigmond 1981.

Cactus Family (Cactaceae)
Beavertail Pricklypear
Opuntia basilaris Engelm. & Bigelow

Figure 101

Owens Valley Paiute: *"neu-bu"* [49]
Southern Paiute: *navump, navumpi* [52]; *navumb* [53]
Timbisha Shoshone: *"navou"* [49]
Western Shoshone: *nugwia* [71];
  "nah-vomb," "wo-gay-be" [78]

Description and Habitat

Beavertail pricklypear is a low-spreading perennial with flat joints [41]. No spines are found on the flat bluish green stems, but a yellowish brown or reddish furze composed of tiny spines (glochids) grows in depressions on the surface of these pads [42]. Flowers are usually brilliant magenta, but can also be white [42]. Plants are widely distributed throughout the region below 5500 feet in creosote bush, saltbush, sagebrush, and, rarely, in pinyon-juniper communities [5].

Native Uses

Traditionally, Western Shoshone people knocked the meaty fruits off the plant with a stick and ate them fresh or dried and stored them for year-round use [71]. Today, Native people still eat cactus fruits fresh or make them into jelly [43]. Owens Valley Paiutes gathered beavertail cactus pads, cooking them in hot ashes or on hot rocks to blister and remove the skin and spines[49]; they then ate the juicy inner pith. Sometimes people ate fresh pads to quench a thirst [53]. Dried pads were boiled with a little salt and eaten [42]. In the spring, both the Timbisha and Kawaiisu collected cactus blossoms and buds to cook and eat [49, 87]. The prickly fuzz from the pads was rubbed into warts to remove the growths [55]. According to Stoffle

Figure 101. Beavertail pricklypear *(Opuntia basilaris)*

et al., people may have transplanted this cactus to increase the crop and spread its distribution [71].

Sources: [5] Beatley 1976; [41] Hickman 1993; [42] Jaeger 1941; [43] Y. Jake, pers. commun.; [49] Kerr 1936; [53] C. Lynch, pers. commun.; [55] V. Miller, pers. commun.; [71] Stoffle et al. 1989; [78] Train et al. 1941; [87] Zigmond 1981.

Cactus Family (Cactaceae)
Mojave Pricklypear
Opuntia erinacea Engelm. & Bigelow ex Engelm.

Figure 102

Southern Paiute: *manavi* [71]

Figure 102. Mojave prick-lypear *(Opuntia erinacea)*

Description and Habitat

The Mojave pricklypear (also known as the grizzlybear pricklypear) has oval or oblong joints and long, shaggy, flexible brown or white spines [41]. The fruit also bears slender spines. Flowers are commonly lemon yellow to bronze, although some plants have reddish purple flowers [42]. Mojave pricklypear grows on gravelly or stony slopes in blackbrush, sagebrush, and pinyon-juniper communities throughout southern Nevada, between 3700 and 7200 feet elevation [5]. It is also found, less commonly, in saltbush communities.

Native Uses

The fruits were eaten fresh and roasted, made into a jam [71] and wine [9], or dried and stored for year-round consumption [71].

Sources: [5] Beatley 1976; [9] Bye 1972; [41] Hickman 1993; [42] Jaeger 1941; [71] Stoffle et al. 1989.

CACTI

Cactus Family (Cactaceae)

Cottontop Cactus

Echinocactus polycephalus Engelm. & Bigelow

Figure 103

Owens Valley Paiute: *"dem-a-cale-nu-pa-ber"* [49]
Southern Paiute: *"thamave"* [53]
Timbisha Shoshone: *"nah-voo"* [49]; *"tah-wimps," "tu-gimb"* (seed) [58]

Description and Habitat

The globular cottontop cactus (also called clustered barrel cactus) grows in clumps of several stems that together may have a diameter of up to 3 feet, each stem being 1–2 feet tall and 5–10 inches in diameter [41]. Stems are distinctly ribbed, with densely clustered spines along each rib. The spines are red or yellow, with thick central spines that measure 2–3 inches long and may be slightly curved [41]. Flowers are 2–3 inches in diameter, yellow tinged with pink, and very fragrant. Flowering in late summer, the cottontop is one of the latest blooming cacti in our area [42]. The woolly ovary of the flower becomes a dry fruit with white fur, giving the cactus the name "cottontop" [42]. Cottontop cactus is frequently found scattered throughout the Mojave Desert below about 5000 feet elevation, growing especially large in creosote bush and shadscale associations on limestone-derived substrates [5].

Figure 103. Cottontop cactus *(Echinocactus polycephalus)*

Native Uses

The sturdy spines of the cottontop cactus served as needles or awls [66, 71, 87]. Among the Kawaiisu, the spine was enclosed in a handle made from creosote bush or sagebrush lac [87]. Cottontop cactus seeds were used for food [42, 49]. According to Mark Kerr, "the plant is baked and ground to a powder and used for burns" by the Owens Valley Paiute [49].

Sources: [5] Beatley 1976; [41] Hickman 1993; [42] Jaeger 1941; [49] Kerr 1936; [53] C. Lynch, pers. commun.; [55] V. Miller, pers. commun.; [58] Murphey 1959; [66] Steward 1938; [71] Stoffle et al. 1989; [87] Zigmond 1981.

Cactus Family (Cactaceae)

Hedgehog Cactus
Echinocereus engelmannii (Parry ex Engelm.) Lemaire

Figure 104

Southern Paiute: *tule* [71]; *wisuyuavimpi* [48]; *"hu-siv-vich"* [53]; *u'sivi, usivwits* [52]
Timbisha Shoshone: *"ovee"* [49]; *"tar-wha-par"* (fruit) [49]

Description and Habitat

The hedgehog cactus consists of dense clusters of columnar or elongated cylindrical stems that grow up to 2 feet tall; each stem is 2–5 inches in diameter and has ten to thirteen prominent ribs [41]. Spines on the ribs are numerous, multicolored, and often quite long, the main ones measuring up to 3 inches in length [42]. Flowers are funnel shaped, rose to lavender in color, and up to 3 inches in diameter [41]. The fruit is fleshy, red, and edible [41]. This cactus is frequently found in desert shrub communities below about 6600 feet elevation [5].

Native Uses

The Southern Paiute gathered hedgehog cactus fruit in late summer and ate it fresh [48]. They also cooked the fleshy stems [48]. Owens Valley Paiute people had not heard of the use of this cactus [49], but the neighboring Timbisha apparently used the fruit either dried or fresh [49]. According to some consultants, the fruit of hedgehog cactus is still eaten fresh today [71].

Figure 104. Hedgehog cactus *(Echinocereus engelmannii)*

Sources: [5] Beatley 1976; [41] Hickman 1993; [42] Jaeger 1941; [48] Kelly 1964; [49] Kerr 1936; [52] Lawlor 1995; [53] C. Lynch, pers. commun.; [71] Stoffle et al. 1989.

CHAPTER SIX

Herbaceous Plants

Lizard's Tail Family (Saururaceae)

Yerba Mansa

Anemopsis californica (Nutt.) Hook. & Arn.

Figure 105

Owens Valley Paiute: *"cha-wan-eba"* [49]; *"nupitchi"* [55]
Southern Paiute: *"chew-pahn-iv"* [78]; *tchupaniv* [71]; *tcupani* [50]; *"ch'ponip"* [58]
Timbisha Shoshone: *"saw-wan-eup"* [49]
Western Shoshone: *"chew-pon-iv"* [78]; *"nupitchi"* [58]

Description and Habitat

Yerba mansa is a low-growing, water-loving perennial herb that bears leathery ovate leaves and conspicuous white flower clusters on terminal stalks about 6 inches high [41]. It prefers moist alkaline areas, principally around springs and wet meadows at Ash Meadows, Oasis Valley, and other localities below 4000 feet in southern Nevada [5].

Native Uses

Yerba mansa is an important medicinal plant that is widely used by Native peoples throughout its range in western North America. The roots are strongly aromatic and peppery in flavor. They were boiled as a tea for use in relieving colds and coughing [87], for recuperation after a cold, for treating stomachache, or as a laxative [65]. A tea made from the boiled plant was used to treat venereal disease [65, 78]. Mashed boiled roots or boiled leaves were used externally as a poultice to relieve swelling, and the decoction also served as an antiseptic wash [78, 87]. The Moapa Paiute boiled the leaves in water to make a soothing bath to ease muscle pains and sore feet [78]. According to modern consultants, one could also put the roots in a bath or in a vaporizer [71]. Among the Owens Valley Paiute, the roots were boiled and a person breathed in the vapors under a cloth cover for relief of asthma [55]. If the roots were roasted and dried, they could be stored indefinitely [87].

Figure 105. Yerba mansa
(Anemopsis californica)

The Southern Paiute use a tea made from the roots for bladder and kidney ailments [53].

Sources: [5] Beatley 1976; [41] Hickman 1993; [48] Kelly 1964; [49] Kerr 1936; [50] Laird 1976; [53] C. Lynch, pers. commun.; [55] V. Miller, pers. commun.; [58] Murphey 1959; [65] Steward 1933; [67] Steward 1941; [70] Stewart 1942; [71] Stoffle et al. 1989; [78] Train et al. 1941; [93] Zigmond 1981.

Sunflower Family (Asteraceae)

Annual Turtleback
Psathyrotes annua (Nutt.) Gray

Velvet Turtleback
Psathyrotes ramosissima (Torr.) Gray

Figure 106

Figure 106. Turtleback *(Psathyrotes ramosissima)*

Owens Valley Paiute: *"sebu magoonobu"* [55]
Southern Paiute: *"sebu magoonobu"* [58]
Western Shoshone: *"yoh-nip," "quoy-hee-nut-zoo"* [78]

Description and Habitat

Turtleback is a low-growing annual or perennial herb that forms a
rounded mound or mat. The mound's surface is composed of woolly ovate
leaves showing prominent veining, with smooth to slightly toothed margins. When crushed, the leaves smell like turpentine [42]. Small orange
flower heads dot the surface of the velvety gray mound of leaves [14, 42].
The annual turtleback *(Psathyrotes annua)* is found in dry, often alkaline
open places in creosote bush, wolfberry, and saltbush desert scrub communities between 2200 and 6000 feet elevation [5, 14]. The velvet turtleback
(Psathyrotes ramosissima) is found in washes in creosote bush communities
up to 3000 feet elevation [5], but is most common in lower deserts such
as Death Valley [42].

Native Uses

Turtleback served a variety of medicinal needs [78]. A brew of the entire
plant eased stomachache in children and helped cure urinary ailments. An
eyewash was made by steeping the dried leaves [55, 58]. The plant decoction
was taken for intestinal disorders, liver trouble, kidney and bladder ailments,
and other diseases [58, 78]. The green plant was crushed and used as a wet
dressing on swellings or snakebites. Chewing the leaves, fresh or dried, could

also relieve toothache [55], and turtleback was often called the "toothache plant" for that reason [58].

Sources: [5] Beatley 1976; [14] Cronquist 1994; [42] Jaeger 1941; [55] V. Miller, pers. commun.; [58] Murphey 1959; [78] Train et al. 1941.

Buckwheat Family (Polygonaceae)
Desert Trumpet
Eriogonum inflatum Torr. & Frém.

Figure 107

Owens Valley Paiute: *hausa'ava* [65]
Southern Paiute: *papa karum(p)* [71]; *papa kumba* [53]; *"babagorum"* [58]
Timbisha Shoshone: *"to-sana-ambow-keep," "o-sana-boa-keep"* [49];
    "tosanan bawkip" [58]
Western Shoshone: *tusarumbokup* [71]

Figure 107. Desert trumpet *(Eriogonum inflatum)*

Description and Habitat

Desert trumpet (also known as desert spoon) is a common and distinctive perennial herb in much of the Mojave Desert [42]. The plant grows 8–32 inches tall [41] from a basal rosette of rounded silvery green leaves [42]. Several bare green tubular stems, topped by a loose network of small branchlets, rise above the basal leaf cluster. The branchlets produce umbels of tiny yellow flowers in the spring and fall. The stems become reddish, dry, and brittle in the fall. The plant is widely distributed, but prefers calcareous soils in creosote bush, blackbrush, saltbush, and sagebrush communities below limestone mountain ranges between 2200 and 5000 feet [5].

Native Uses

Fresh, fat young stems of the desert trumpet were eaten raw [62, 71]. The Timbisha sometimes ate the roots [49], and seeds were eaten by the Kawaiisu [87]. When dried, the inflated stems served as pipes for smoking tobacco [58, 71, 87] and as children's toys. Boys would pretend to smoke dirt in toy pipes made from the swollen stalk [65]. One consultant reported that tiny black "seeds" (actually insect droppings) were used as a medicine, but only in the right dosage, because large quantities were reputedly hallucinogenic [71].

Sources: [5] Beatley 1976; [41] Hickman 1993; [42] Jaeger 1941; [49] Kerr 1936; [53] C. Lynch, pers. commun.; [58] Murphey 1959; [62] Palmer 1878; [65] Steward 1933; [71] Stoffle et al. 1989; [87] Zigmond 1981.

Four O'Clock Family (Nyctaginaceae)

Transmontane Sand Verbena
Abronia turbinata Torr. ex S. Wats.

Desert Sand Verbena
Abronia villosa S. Wats.

Figures 108, 109

Owens Valley Paiute: *"ayaho"* [55]
Southern Paiute: *"ayaho"* [58]
Western Shoshone: *"nut-zooh-boh-hombe," "bah-gun-boh-hombe"* [78]

Description and Habitat

Sand verbena is a low-growing winter annual with a trailing stem, sticky rounded leaves, and showy globular clusters of white or pink flowers that

Figure 108. Transmontane sand verbena *(Abronia turbinata)*

Figure 109. Desert sand verbena *(Abronia villosa)*

possess a delicate fragrance [42]. It is usually found growing in deep loose volcanic sands and dunes, along drainages, or on gentle slopes below about 5500 feet elevation [5]. The white-flowered transmontane sand verbena *(Abronia turbinata)* generally grows above 3500 feet elevation, in association with both warm- and cool-desert shrub associations including those dominated by creosote bush–burrobush, wolfberry–spiny hopsage, shadscale, and sagebrush [5]. The pink-flowered desert sand verbena (*Abronia villosa*) grows at lower elevations (below 3500 feet elevation) and further south in the Mojave Desert and is usually associated with creosote bush scrub [5, 42].

Native Uses

Several Native groups in the Great Basin used sand verbenas as a medicinal plant [78]. The name of one of these species, *"nut-zooh-boh-hombe,"* reflects this usage by including the Western Shoshone term for medicine, *natsu* or "nut-zoo" [11]. The sticky leaves of the white sand verbena were applied externally to reduce swellings, and the root of the pink sand verbena was mashed and made into a moist poultice to relieve burns. The Moapa Southern Paiute used the desert sand verbena as a diuretic in the treatment of kidney and bladder ailments [58].

Sources: [5] Beatley 1976; [11] Chamberlin 1911; [42] Jaeger 1941; [55] V. Miller, pers. commun.; [58] Murphey 1959; [78] Train et al. 1941.

Evening Primrose Family (Onagraceae)

Evening Primrose
Oenothera spp., *Camissonia* spp.

Figures 110, 111

Owens Valley Paiute: *ko'do'ova* [65]; *"nac-a-go-av"* [49];
"koatsa dobe buha" [55]
Timbisha Shoshone: *"sea-gowa-ta," "sea-wah-ta"* [49]; *"tee-wah-tah"* [49]

Description and Habitat

The Mojave Desert is home to numerous species of evening primrose in two main genera, *Camissonia* and *Oenothera*. All are annual or perennial herbs, usually having showy flowers composed of four white, rose, or yellow petals that generally open at dusk during the spring to summer months [18, 42]. Plants often have a rosette of basal leaves, above which rise numerous flowering stems (such as Booth's evening primrose, *Camissonia boothii*). Alterna-tively, some evening primroses (such as Hooker's evening primrose, *Oenothera elata* ssp. *hirsutissima*) have a single stout stem crowded with leaves and flowers. The fruit is a linear or oval capsule that is often woody and contains many small seeds [18]. Species of evening primrose typically grow in open gravelly or sandy soils, often near washes or disturbed sites, but they are also common on alluvial hills and flats [5, 42]. In years with adequate

Figure 110. Desert sun cup *(Camissonia brevipes)*

Figure 111. Sand-lily *(Oenothera caespitosa)*

HERBACEOUS PLANTS   121

moisture, evening primroses can carpet Mojave Desert valleys in an astonishing show of gold or cream. Among the species found in the region are the yellow-flowered Mojave sun cup *(Camissonia campestris)*, with erect flowering stems, and the low-growing tufted evening primrose *(Oenothera caespitosa* ssp. *marginata)*, with large white flowers. Hooker's evening primrose, a plant with known ethnobotanical value, grows in moist meadows in southern Nevada and at higher elevations in the Great Basin to the north [5, 18].

Native Uses

The Timbisha Shoshone of Death Valley and the Owens Valley Paiute collected seeds of Hooker's evening primrose. These seeds were ground to a meal and eaten raw [49, 65] or toasted [56].

Sources: [5] Beatley 1976; [18] Cronquist et al. 1997; [42] Jaeger 1941; [49] Kerr 1936; [55] V. Miller, pers. commun.; [56] B. Moose, pers. commun.; [65] Steward 1933.

Nightshade Family (Solanaceae)

Thorn Apple
Datura wrightii Regel

Figure 112

Owens Valley Paiute: *tanganiva* [65]; *"tar-nar-neva," "main-oph-wuh"* [49]
Southern Paiute: *momomp* [71]; *momompi* [50]; *mimip* [47];
  momipi [47, 48]; *moh-mope* [78]; *"main-oph-weep," "man-op-weep,"*
  "man-oph-weep" [9]; *"tolache"* [58]
Western Shoshone: *"moip"* [58]; *"moh-eep"* [78]

Description and Habitat:

Thorn apple (also known as jimson weed) is an annual or perennial plant about 2 feet high and 3 feet across, with large dark green deltoid leaves and white funnel-shaped flowers suffused with violet [41, 42]. The large leaves and flowers are a rarity in the desert, making the plant very conspicuous. The fruit is a round leathery capsule that measures about 1 inch in diameter and is covered with prickles [41]. The plant dies back in winter but often grows back from the rootstock with the return of warmer weather in spring. Sacred datura grows in major sandy or gravelly washes and disturbed areas, in association with creosote bush and rabbitbrush below about 4200 feet elevation [5].

HERBACEOUS PLANTS

Figure 112. Thorn Apple *(Datura wrightii)* in flower

Native Uses

The alkaloids of sacred datura have strong hallucinogenic properties, and for that reason it was sometimes used to undertake a vision or dream quest [71]. A vision seeker would roast or bake the roots, grind them to a powder, mix it with water, and drink a small amount of the decoction to induce the hallucinogenic state. Sometimes such a quest was undertaken as part of the process toward becoming a shaman [48]. The initiate took datura under the guidance of an experienced shaman or spiritual guide [65, 71]. Such guidance was important, because ingesting too large a dose could easily prove fatal, and the guide could protect the initiate from harm during the dream state [49, 65, 71, 87]. The trance induced wandering, the wanderer being accompanied by a "guard who whistled to call him back" [65].

Datura could be used to help cure sickness, visit dead relatives, predict the future, see visions of past events, or find lost objects [48, 49, 65]. Among the Las Vegas Southern Paiute, datura was used for finding lost objects, but not as a source of shamanistic power [47]. The Pahranagat Southern Paiute and Western Shoshone did not consider datura a way to become a shaman, although it was used to locate lost items because the person under its influence could "see through things" [47, 67]. It was also used to "see the future" [43]. Some ate a few seeds for help in gambling [65] or to obtain a narcotic high [9, 47].

Thorn apple was much feared and used sparingly, however. According to one report from Owens Valley, "this plant was seldom used as the partaker either died or became violently insane. One informant only remembered one incident of its use, and the user became incurably insane" [49]. The Kawaiisu used sacred datura only in winter, after the leaves and flowers had died back; otherwise, it would be too strong and dangerous [87]. Some consultants expressly denied that their group used it [53].

Thorn apple also has important medicinal qualities. For the Kawaiisu, it was considered one of the four original medicines given to people, along with tobacco (*Nicotiana* spp.), nettles (*Urtica* spp.), and red ants [87]. Water in which the root of thorn apple had soaked was used as an external medicine for arthritis or was drunk for broken bones or bad wounds. The Las Vegas Southern Paiute used it as a medicine for rheumatism [47]. One person in Owens Valley thought that the local datura had no value because it grew near human habitations and that the good powerful plants must be gathered from the unoccupied parts of the Mojave Desert [65].

Sources: [5] Beatley 1976; [9] Bye 1972; [41] Hickman 1993; [42] Jaeger 1941; [43] Y. Jake, pers. commun.; [47] Kelly 1939; [48] Kelly 1964; [49] Kerr 1936; [50] Laird 1976; [53] C. Lynch, pers. commun.; [58] Murphey 1959; [65] Steward 1933; [67] Steward 1941; [71] Stoffle et al. 1989; [87] Zigmond 1981.

Nightshade Family (Solanaceae)

Desert Tobacco
Nicotiana obtusifolia Mertens & Galleotti

Coyote Tobacco
Nicotiana attenuata Torr. ex S. Wats.

Figures 113, 114

Owens Valley Paiute: *pamüpi* [65]; *"sow-a-wan-pee"* (whole plant) [49]; *"pam-pee"* (tobacco) [49]

Southern Paiute: *saxwaxwapi* [71]; *sagwog-woapɨ* [48]; *"sawak wape"* [58]; *koʔʷa, sagwakoʷap* [50]; *ko'üp* [65]; *"ko-a-pe"* [53]; *"tsaw-wap"* [33]

Timbisha Shoshone: *pahumbi* [65]; *soh'guhu* [25]

Western Shoshone: *pombi* [71]; *"poo-ee-pah," "new-wha bah-hoon," "pue-bax"* [78]; *"pwui bamo"* (green tobacco), *"bahombe"* (cured tobacco) [58]

Description and Habitat

Desert tobacco *(Nicotiana obtusifolia)* is a 1- to 5-foot tall biennial or perennial with a woody base and sticky, dark green triangular leaves [16, 41]. Its greenish white tubular flowers are nearly 1 inch long. It grows on limestone substrates between 2600 and 4800 feet elevation in rocky canyons and

Figure 113. Desert to-
bacco *(Nicotiana
obtusifolia)*

washes, although it can often be found on ledges or at the base of cliffs in
creosote bush and saltbush communities [5].

Coyote tobacco *(Nicotiana attenuata)*, an annual, ranges from 1 to 6 feet
high. Its white tubular flowers are 1–2 inches long. It grows on volcanic substrates chiefly in canyons and usually along ledges or at the base of cliffs.
This plant is also found on disturbed sites. Coyote tobacco grows with sagebrush, pinyon, and juniper between 3500 and 7500 feet elevation.

Native Uses

Wild tobacco was an important and valued plant. The leaves were smoked
for medicine, ceremony, and pleasure [71]. Tobacco is one of the four original medicines given to people, according to the Kawaiisu, along with *Datura*,
nettles (*Urtica* sp.), and red ants [87]. The tobacco that the Kawaiisu used
was a different species, Indian tobacco *(Nicotiana quadrivalvis)*, which was
very strong medicine indeed, and it was tended and gathered with care. The
species found in southern Nevada, desert and coyote tobacco, were much
weaker and inferior plants, used only when Indian tobacco was not available.

HERBACEOUS PLANTS

Figure 114. Coyote tobacco
(Nicotiana attenuata)

In Owens Valley, tobacco plants were not sown, but plots were cleared, burned and, tended and plants were irrigated during droughts [65]. Tobacco plants were pruned to encourage the growth of larger leaves. Among the Timbisha Shoshone and the Southern Paiute, plots were burned to clear them for sowing, but the plants *(N. attenuata)* were not watered or weeded [33, 48].

Leaves were gathered in late summer, dried, ground, moistened with water, and made into balls measuring 12–16 inches in diameter. Plugs cut from the balls, called *"so-go"* by the Owens Valley Paiute [49, 56], were smoked sparingly, usually by older men [65]. Women chewed tobacco mixed with ashes from the fire or with lime made from burning shells; they used it while gambling or gossiping, but it was bad for the teeth [56]. The Timbisha roasted leaves with snail shells or other sources of lime. Older people put a small amount of tobacco under the tongue to stimulate the heart, although the wrong use caused dizziness [25]. Tobacco was sometimes mixed with leaves or bark from other plants for smoking. Moapa Paiute people smoked tobacco mixed with a species of mistletoe (possibly *Phoradendron californicum*) that lives on creosote bush, using pipes made from the desert trumpet *(Eriogonum inflatum)* [58].

Tobacco plugs were an important trade item, and even tobacco juice "after solidification was often used in trade" [49]. In historic times, wild tobacco was smoked when commercial tobacco was unavailable [9]. The Southern Paiute traded wild tobacco growing in its territory with neighboring groups, such as the Mohave. "A lot of tobacco came from near Las Vegas," one informant told anthropologist William Wallace [81]. "Sometimes two, three, or even four men would go up there and get leaves. Sometimes they would get seeds too. They brought back big bundles of leaves, enough to go around until the next crop. There is still lots of tobacco up there." People gathering wild tobacco pretended to quarrel with one another as they approached the plants to make the leaves stronger.

Native doctors sometimes smoked tobacco as part of the curing rites. Others exhaled smoke to blow away disease. Some believed that smoking the leaves helped cure colds, asthma, or tuberculosis [78]. Ground tobacco leaves mixed with water, Mormon tea *(Ephedra),* and a soft white stone (called *tina'bi* by the Southern Paiute) was used as a strong emetic [47, 49, 65, 78]. Anthropologist Isabel Kelly recorded this use among the Southern Paiute in the 1930s: The above mixture was "made into a paste and placed in [the] center of [a] circle of ailing persons. Each of [the] latter dipped [a] finger into [the] mess, taking [a] small taste. Vomiting followed shortly" [47]. The Southern Paiute and other groups used wild tobacco to help cure external wounds or deep cuts. Tobacco leaves were chewed or mixed with water, and the juice was dripped into the cut, which was then covered with tobacco leaves [47, 65, 78].

Sources: [5] Beatley 1976; [9] Bye 1972; [16] Cronquist et al. 1984; [25] P. Esteves, pers. commun.; [33] Fowler 1996; [34] Fowler and Fowler 1971; [41] Hickman 1993; [47] Kelly 1939; [48] Kelly 1964; [49] Kerr 1936; [50] Laird 1976; [53] C. Lynch, pers. commun.; [56] B. Moose, pers. commun.; [58] Murphey 1959; [65] Steward 1933; [71] Stoffle et al. 1989; [78] Train et al. 1941; [81] Wallace 1953; [87] Zigmond 1981.

Milkweed Family (Asclepiadaceae)

Desert Milkweed
Asclepias erosa Torr.

Mexican Whorled Milkweed
Asclepias fascicularis Dcne.

Showy Milkweed

Asclepias speciosa Torr.

Figures 115, 116

Owens Valley Paiute: *"wishe-veu-eup," "kuts-a-hon-i-pea"*
(for *Asclepias speciosa*), *"oo-m-p"* (for *Asclepias fascicularis*) [49];
avanava (for *Asclepias speciosa*) [65]
Timbisha Shoshone: *"sana-go-vee," "tim-be-wechave"* [49]

Description and Habitat

Milkweed is a tall perennial herb that reaches 3 feet or more in height [16, 41]. Its lanceolate-ovate leaves with saw-edged margins clasp the stem. When broken, the stem and leaves exude a characteristic white sap (the milk) that contains latex, a natural rubber. On top of the stem are umbels of small, greenish white flowers, each divided into five segments, with each individual segment looking somewhat like a goblet or hourglass. Long pointed woody seed capsules are attached to silky plumes (the coma). Desert milkweed *(Asclepias erosa)* is found in sandy washes in a wide range of elevations from low desert to the juniper zone [5]. Mexican whorled milkweed *(Asclepias fascicularis)* is found in moist areas at low elevations below 3400 feet, such as Ash Meadows and Oasis Valley [5]. Showy milkweed *(Asclepias speciosa)* is rare in southern Nevada and more common in the Great Basin to the north [16].

Native Uses

Margaret Wheat [83] noted that, "lacking nails, bolts, and screws, and having little to use for adhesives, the Paiute Indians tied their world together." Milkweed was one of the most important native fiber sources, used to make string, nets, textiles, clothing, mats, and other items. Mexican whorled milkweed and showy milkweed were most often used for making fiber, but desert milkweed was used as well [87]. Showy milkweed was generally used for fine string, whereas Mexican whorled milkweed was best for stouter twine to make rabbit nets and other articles [49].

To make the string, milkweed stems were cut off at the base when dry (around August). The very fine fibers were obtained from dried stems by scraping away the outer skin and inner pith. These fibers were then dipped in water and quickly rolled on the leg to make twisted two- or three-ply twine that was very fine, soft, and strong.

The milky latex was also useful as a medicine and a chewing gum. The latex served as an antiseptic and healing agent for sores and cuts. It was also used to remove corns and calluses. To make gum, the bitter latex was either boiled until thick or dried, then washed several times; it was then ready for chewing [49, 87]. At first, the gum was bitter and the juice was spat out, but it later sweetened. The Timbisha term for this chewing gum is *"sana-go-vee"*

Figure 115. Desert milkweed *(Asclepias erosa)*

Figure 116. Showy milk-
weed *(Asclepias speciosa)*

[49]. The Western Shoshone around Beatty rolled the milk in the hand until it was hard enough for chewing; the gum was called *"samoko"* [58]. The mashed root of milkweed, moistened with water, made a poultice for swellings. Hot tea made from boiled roots was used for respiratory diseases and other maladies. The seeds were used as a salve for sores or in a boiled decoction to draw the poison out of rattlesnake bites [78].

According to anthropologist Julian Steward [65], the Owens Valley Paiute ate the seeds of showy milkweed. Cronquist et al. [16] stated that "Indians ate the stems, leaves, flowers and young fruits after removing the bitter sap by boiling. The young, tender stalks are said to be eaten as greens, tasting somewhat like asparagus stalks."

Sources: [5] Beatley 1976; [16] Cronquist et al. 1984; [41] Hickman 1993; [49] Kerr 1936; [58] Murphey 1959; [65] Steward 1933; [78] Train et al. 1941; [83] Wheat 1967; [87] Zigmond 1981.

Dogbane Family (Apocynaceae)

Indian Hemp

Apocynum cannabinum L.

Figure 117

Owens Valley Paiute: *"wishe-vevah," "wishe-varva"* [49]; *"we-ha"* [55]
Southern Paiute: *w'ivi* [48]; *wö'iv^i* [70]
Western Shoshone: *wana* [66]

Description and Habitat

Indian hemp is a stout perennial herb that grows to 1–4 feet tall [16]. Large ovate to lanceolate leaves with pointed tips are arranged opposite each other on the stems. The leaves and stems exude a milky white sap when broken, like the milkweeds (*Asclepias* spp.). Small white or greenish flowers, which appear in midsummer, mature to narrow pendulous fruits that are 4–8 inches long and contain numerous seeds marked with tufts of long hairs [16]. Indian hemp grows in damp areas near springs and along washes. It is found at Ash Meadows and in moist areas in sagebrush and pinyon-juniper plant associations in the higher mountains of the region [5].

Native Uses

Indian hemp was one of the most important native sources of fiber, used to make twine and cordage for a wide variety of purposes [22]. After the stems were soaked in water, fibers and bark were easily removed. A little more

Figure 117. Indian hemp
(Apocynum cannabinum)

washing to remove the bark left soft, fine yellowish brown silks of considerable strength and durability. Long nets used in rabbit drives were made of this twine; it took a month of work to make a rabbit net [48]. Once the rabbits were caught and skinned, Indian hemp cordage went into making rabbitskin blankets, an important article of clothing for Great Basin peoples [48, 67, 70]. Cordage made from Indian hemp has been found in several archaeological sites in the southern Great Basin and Mojave Desert [19]. In the northern Great Basin, Indian hemp bark was mixed with tobacco for smoking [66].

The Shoshone name for this plant, *wana*, is similar to *wasn*, their name for string or net, and undoubtedly reflects the same root term [66]. Among the Owens Valley Paiute, the name *"wishe-vevah"* refers to "something to make string with" [49]. The name is given to Indian hemp as well as to milkweed *(Asclepias* spp.) and woolly bluestar *(Amsonia tomentosa)*, other important fiber sources.

Sources: [5] Beatley 1976; [16] Cronquist et al. 1984; [19] Davis and Smith 1981; [22] Ebeling 1986; [48] Kelly 1964; [49] Kerr 1936; [55] V. Miller, pers. commun.; [66] Steward 1938; [67] Steward 1941; [70] Stewart 1942.

Dogbane Family (Apocynaceae)

Woolly Bluestar

Amsonia tomentosa Torr. & Frém.

Figure 118

Owens Valley Paiute: *wiciva* [65]

Description and Habitat

This perennial subshrub produces many erect herbaceous stems that grow to 8–24 inches high from a woody base [16, 41]. When broken, these stems exude a milky juice [42]. The grayish green leaves and fruits are smaller, narrower, and less conspicuous than those of its relative Indian hemp *(Apocynum cannabinum)*, but the branches of woolly bluestar bear a wealth of white to sky blue flowers in late spring. Woolly bluestar is uncommon and is typically restricted to dry gravelly soils near washes in or below limestone mountain ranges [5]. It grows between 2200 and 3800 feet elevation in desert shrub communities associated with saltbush, blackbrush, and *Ephedra* [5].

Figure 118. Woolly bluestar *(Amsonia tomentosa)*

Native Uses

Like Indian hemp, the stems of woolly bluestar yielded strong fibers. These were braided together to make carrying straps and twine. A two-ply cord made from this material was used in the construction of rabbitskin blankets [20]. The milk from the stems was used as a laxative among the Owens Valley Paiute [56].

Sources: [5] Beatley 1976; [16] Cronquist et al. 1984; [20] DeDecker 1984; [41] Hickman 1993; [42] Jaeger 1941; [56] B. Moose, pers. commun.; [65] Steward 1933.

Mustard Family (Brassicaceae)
Entireleaved Thelypody
Thelypodium integrifolium (Nutt.) Endl. ex Walp.

Figure 119

Owens Valley Paiute: *"huma"* [55]
Southern Paiute: *nambitu* [71]; *"na-bita"* [53]

Figure 119. Entireleaved thelypody *(Thelypodium integrifolium)*

Description and Habitat

This mustard is a biennial herb that grows from a basal rosette of thick oblong leaves; its single erect stem measures 3–5 feet high [41, 42]. The thick stem bears lanceolate leaves and, at the top, a dense spike of greenish white flowers that are sometimes tinged with purple. Fruits are thin up-curved pods (siliques) that are about 1–2 inches long and full of tiny seeds [41]. Entireleaved thelypody is common in sandy, silty, and alkaline areas associated with mesquite and saltbush in the vicinity of Ash Meadows and other low-lying well-watered valley areas [5].

Native Uses

The young leaves and stems of entireleaved thelypody were boiled and eaten as greens [53]. The plants were harvested to ensure two or three good crops per year and a continually reliable supply [71].

Sources: [5] Beatley 1976; [41] Hickman 1993; [42] Jaeger 1941; [53] C. Lynch, pers. commun.; [55] V. Miller, pers. commun.; [71] Stoffle et al. 1989.

Mustard Family (Brassicaceae)
Desert Rockcress
Arabis pulchra M. E. Jones ex S. Wats.

Figure 120

Southern Paiute: *ak, akh* [71]

Description and Habitat

Desert rockcress is a perennial wild mustard with a somewhat woody base and stems that grow to 8–24 inches tall [41]. Short gray hairs cover the leaves and stems. Leaves are generally clustered at the base of the plant and grow more sparingly up the stem. Showy purple-rose flowers with four petals bloom on spikes 10–18 inches high [41]. The flowers later form flat downward-hanging pods that measure 2 inches long and are covered with small star-shaped hairs [42].

Desert rockcress is common on rocky hillsides and almost always grows under the shade and dripline of other shrubs [5]. It is widely distributed in southern Nevada at 3500–7500 feet elevation [5]. Desert rockcress is found most commonly in blackbrush, sagebrush, and pinyon-juniper plant associations and less frequently in association with creosote bush or saltbush [5].

HERBACEOUS PLANTS

Figure 120. Desert rock-cress *(Arabis pulchra)*

Native Uses

As with other mustards, the tiny seeds of desert rockcress were sometimes collected for food [71]. Crushed plants of a related species, silver rockcress *(Arabis puberula)*, were used as a liniment or mustard plaster [78].

Sources: [5] Beatley 1976; [41] Hickman 1993; [42] Jaeger 1941; [71] Stoffle et al. 1989; [78] Train et al. 1941.

Mustard Family (Brassicaceae)
Tansy Mustard
Descurainia pinnata (Walt.) Britt.

Figure 121

Owens Valley Paiute: *atsa* [49, 66]

Figure 121. Tansy mustard
(Descurainia pinnata)

Southern Paiute: *ku'u, akh'* [71]; *ak, aka vu* [66]; *'aka* [50]; *akive* [53]; *akɨ* [48]; *"ok"* [9]; *"hahck"* [9]
Timbisha Shoshone: *"poin-yah"* [49]
Western Shoshone: *poyah* [71]; *poina, boina* [66]

Description and Habitat

Tansy mustard is an erect branched annual that grows to 6–24 inches tall, with finely dissected leaves and small pale greenish yellow flowers [41]. Each flower forms a long narrow pod with many yellowish to brown seeds arranged in two rows. Tansy mustard is abundant on loose soil over rodent burrows, roadsides, and in other disturbed areas in virtually all plant communities below about 9000 feet elevation [5].

Native Uses

Tansy mustard was a valued food plant [66, 71]. In spring the stems and leaves were boiled as greens [9, 66, 71]. In summer, the small seeds were gathered into baskets or blankets with a seed-beater. The seeds were parched with hot coals in a basket, ground fine, and the flour was mixed with water to make a beverage [87], mush, or soup, sometimes in combination with other seeds [9]. People used the flour to make a type of bread. The seeds were a good condiment and were added to other foods as a spice or to disguise other flavors [9]. Among the Southern Paiute, tansy mustard seeds were sometimes "mixed with snow as [a] confection" [48]. The seeds were stored whole or ground for year-round use [49, 71].

Sources: [5] Beatley 1976; [9] Bye 1972; [41] Hickman 1993; [48] Kelly 1964; [49] Kerr 1936; [50] Laird 1976; [53] C. Lynch, pers. commun.; [66] Steward 1938; [71] Stoffle et al. 1989; [87] Zigmond 1981.

Mustard Family (Brassicaceae)
Heartleaf Twistflower
Streptanthus cordatus Nutt.

Figure 122

Figure 122. Heartleaf twistflower *(Streptanthus cordatus)*

Description and Habitat

Heartleaf twistflower (also called jewelflower) is a stout-stemmed perennial that grows to 1–3 feet high [41]. Its thick basal leaves are heart shaped and clasp the stem. The flower is thick and urn shaped, with the upper part maroon and the lower part of the urn lemon yellow [42]. Seeds are borne in erect narrow pods (silicles). Heartleaf twistflower is common in sagebrush and pinyon-juniper communities above 5000 feet elevation in southern Nevada [5].

Native Uses

The seeds were gathered and eaten in summer [71]. Greens were cooked as potherbs, with several changes of water being used to remove the bitterness [49].

Sources: [5] Beatley 1976; [41] Hickman 1993; [42] Jaeger 1941; [49] Kerr 1936; [71] Stoffle et al. 1989.

Mint Family (Lamiaceae)

Chia

Salvia columbariae Benth.

Figure 123

Owens Valley Paiute: *pacita* [55, 71]; *pasida, pazida* [65]; *"paseda"* [49]
Southern Paiute: *pasiits* [71]; *pasits* [53]
Timbisha Shoshone: *"paseda"* [49]
Western Shoshone: *pacita* [71]

Description and Habitat

Chia is an annual herb that grows to 6–20 inches in height, with fringed leaves usually on the base and lower portion of the square stems [16]. Dense rounded heads of bright blue or purplish flowers ring the upper parts of the stems [16, 41]. The plant is widely distributed but common only locally, preferring disturbed soils such as sandy washes or steep talus slopes in blackbrush, sagebrush, and lower elevations of pinyon-juniper communities at elevations between 2900 and 6000 feet [5]. Chia also grows occasionally with creosote bush and saltbush.

HERBACEOUS PLANTS

Figure 123. Chia *(Salvia columbariae)*

Native Uses

Chia seeds were an important food and were especially favored for mush [71]. Seeds were gathered in spring and early summer after the flowers had dried. Seeds were collected into a basket using a seed-beater [87], or whole plants were gathered when dry and the seeds then threshed out [65]. Roasted chia seeds were ground and mixed with water for a nutritious thick beverage or mush, having a taste similar to milk [49, 87]. The mush was highly nutritious and satisfying: A tablespoonful of seeds was said to suffice for a day's food in lean times [87]. Seeds were also used as an eye medicine; a couple of whole or ground seeds were placed in the eye to relieve irritation [87].

Sources: [5] Beatley 1976; [16] Cronquist et al. 1984; [41] Hickman 1993; [49] Kerr 1936; [50] Laird 1976; [53] C. Lynch, pers. commun.; [55] V. Miller, pers. commun.; [65] Steward 1933; [71] Stoffle et al. 1989; [87] Zigmond 1981.

Loasa Family (Loasaceae)

Whitestem Blazingstar

Mentzelia albicaulis (Dougl. ex Hook.) Dougl. ex Torr. & Gray

Figure 124

Owens Valley Paiute: *"coin-yeuh," "coo-hah"* [49]
Southern Paiute: *ku²u* [48]; *"ko-ka"* [53]; *ko', ku:'ᵘ* [66]; *ku u* [48]
Timbisha Shoshone: *"ko-ah"* [49]
Western Shoshone: *kuha, kuhwa* [66]; *pacita, kua* [71]

Description and Habitat

Whitestem blazingstar (also known as stickleaf) is a widely distributed annual herb that grows up to 16 inches tall, with slender white spreading stems, linear-sinuate leaves covered with sticky hairs, and abundant small bright yellow flowers [41, 42]. The seeds are in sticky tubelike capsules that measure about 1 inch long. Whitestem blazingstar grows between 3600 and 6800 feet in dry sandy or gravelly soil [5]. It grows in numerous plant communities, including creosote bush–burrobush–wolfberry, saltbush, blackbrush, sagebrush, and occasionally sagebrush-pinyon-juniper [5].

Native Uses

The small seeds of whitestem blazingstar were an important food item for Great Basin people. Seed capsules were gathered in spring or early summer

Figure 124. Whitestem blazingstar *(Mentzelia albicaulis)*

HERBACEOUS PLANTS

after the flowers had fallen. They were dried on flat rocks and then threshed and winnowed [49, 66, 87]. The seeds were then parched in a basket tray with coals and ground on a metate. The oily seeds made a rich and nutritious paste about the consistency of peanut butter. Large quantities of seeds were sometimes stored for eventual processing and use [49, 87], or the processed paste was made into "balls about the size of two fists" and stored for later use [87].

The anthropologist Maurice Zigmond [86] reported that the Kawaiisu also used seeds of whitestem blazingstar in making pottery: "The clay pots are filled with *ku'u* preliminary to firing; without the seeds the pots would 'crack and fall apart.'" However, Elizabeth Lawlor [52] warned that such a practice might cause thermal shock during firing and lead to more cracking, not less. She suggested that the oily stickleaf seeds might be used after firing to create a waterproof inner coating.

Sources: [5] Beatley 1976; [41] Hickman 1993; [42] Jaeger 1941; [48] Kelly 1964; [49] Kerr 1936; [52] Lawlor 1995; [53] C. Lynch, pers. commun.; [66] Steward 1938; [86] Zigmond 1941; [87] Zigmond 1981.

Borage Family (Boraginaceae)
Bristly Fiddleneck
Amsinckia tessellata Gray

Figure 125

Owens Valley Paiute: *kuha, kua* [55, 71]; *"ceuh-hava," "kay-heupa"* [49]
Southern Paiute: *"tho-wa-wi-ve"* [53]
Timbisha Shoshone: *tovän'up* [12]
Western Shoshone: *"kuhwa," "tso-hamp"* [11]

Description and Habitat

Bristly fiddleneck is an annual herb that grows about 2 feet high, with dark green lanceolate leaves covered with small bristly hairs [16, 41]. The flower head is curled into a scroll, resembling the end of a violin neck; hence its common name. The small bright yellow flowers bloom in spring and early summer. Fiddleneck is very common in Mojave Desert shrub communities, including the creosote bush–burrobush, wolfberry–spiny hopsage, blackbrush, and sagebrush associations [5]. It is especially common on upper alluvial fans and hills [42]. Fiddleneck is often a dominant spring-flowering annual plant that covers large areas [42].

Figure 125. Bristly
fiddleneck *(Amsinckia
tesselata)*

Native Uses

Bristly fiddleneck was an important source of greens in the spring. Young
stems and leaves were gathered to be used as greens, either cooked or eaten
raw with a little salt [49, 53, 87]. When the sharp bristles developed later,
the leaves were no longer edible. According to some consultants, the plant is
still used by Owens Valley Paiute people [71].

By some accounts, the seeds were also collected for food [71], at least in
the Owens Valley [56]. Stoffle et al. [71] asserted that *kuha* seeds were
stored for later use and may have been broadcast-sown to increase the
abundance of the next year's harvest. However, whether fiddleneck is *kuha*
is uncertain. The Owens Valley Paiute called whitestem blazingstar *(Mentzelia albicaulis)* by this name, and that plant was a well-known and highly
valued small-seed food crop [49, 65, 66, 71]. Thus, fiddleneck may have
been mistaken for blazingstar. Moreover, fiddleneck seeds contain pyr-
rolizidine, a dangerous alkaloid with hallucinogenic properties that is toxic

to livestock and probably to humans as well [60]. Therefore, eating fiddle-neck seeds may be dangerous. Use of fiddleneck seeds as a ritual hallucino-gen has been suggested [60], but accounts from the Owens Valley and elsewhere in the Great Basin do not mention any medicinal or ritual uses for fiddleneck seeds.

Sources: [5] Beatley 1976; [11] Chamberlin 1911; [12] Coville 1892; [16] Cronquist et al. 1984; [41] Hickman 1993; [42] Jaeger 1941; [49] Kerr 1936; [53] C. Lynch, pers. commun.; [55] V. Miller, pers. commun.; [56] B. Moose, pers. commun.; [60] O'Donnell et al. 1997; [65] Steward 1933; [66] Steward 1938; [71] Stoffle et al. 1989; [87] Zigmond 1981.

Buttercup Family (Ranunculaceae)
Desert Larkspur
Delphinium parishii Gray

Figure 126

Owens Valley Paiute: *"coh-hava"* [49]
Timbisha Shoshone: *"multiko"* [58]

Description and Habitat

The desert larkspur is an erect perennial herb that generally grows to 2–3 feet tall, with palmately lobed leaves at the base and lower stem [41] and "light but lively sky blue" spurred flowers along the upper stem [42]. It is found scat-tered under bushes or in rock outcrops in a wide variety of shrub-dominated plant associations between 3000 and 6500 feet elevation [5].

Native Uses

Among the Kawaiisu, larkspur roots were dried, ground, and mixed with water to make a salve for swollen limbs [87]. According to some consultants, however, desert larkspur was regarded as a poisonous plant to be avoided [53, 71], although one ethnographic report from Owens Valley and Death Valley [49] suggested that desert larkspur might have been used for food. Mark Kerr, an amateur botanist and ethnographer working in Owens Valley in the 1930s, reported that the "sweet" seeds of larkspur were eaten raw by the Owens Valley Paiute [49]. The Timbisha Shoshone ground and cooked the seeds and ate the young leaves raw with a little salt. The Timbisha called the seeds *"mo-gaht"* and leaves were *"mer-to-ko,"* according to Kerr [49]. Be-cause some larkspur species are extremely deadly for cattle and other live-stock and because Kerr's account is not verified by other reports, the use of

Figure 126. Desert lark-
spur *(Delphinium parishii)*

larkspur as food must be regarded as uncertain. Given this uncertainty, eating larkspur seeds or leaves is probably unwise and could lead to tragic
results.

Sources: [5] Beatley 1976; [41] Hickman 1993; [42] Jaeger 1941; [49] Kerr 1936;
[53] C. Lynch, pers. commun.; [58] Murphey 1959; [71] Stoffle et al. 1989;
[87] Zigmond 1981.

Figwort Family (Scrophulariaceae)
Indian Paintbrush
Castilleja angustifolia (Nutt.) G. Don

Figure 127

Owens Valley Paiute: *"dosh mooye hanguna"* [55]

Figure 127. Indian paintbrush *(Castilleja angustifolia)*

Southern Paiute: *anabimotoymup* [66]; *"inip-ma-tho-rup"* [53]
Timbisha Shoshone: *anga kwiwi'tum* [66]
Western Shoshone: *angawitam bu* [71]; *"taqua-winnop,"*
   "doo wan dayem" [58]

Description and Habitat

This perennial herb grows to about 8–20 inches high, usually under the protective shade of a larger shrub such as blackbrush [16, 41]. It is conspicuous by its brilliantly colored flower clusters, which appear as a blaze of deep pink to scarlet hues across the desert in spring and summer [42]. Indian paintbrush is found in most shrubby plant associations of lower and middle elevations up to about 6000 feet, including creosote bush, shadscale, blackbrush, and sagebrush communities [5].

Native Uses

A related species, Wyoming Indian paintbrush *(Castilleja linariifolia),* was "prized particularly as a remedy for venereal diseases. . . . The Beatty Indians travel long distances to secure the plant" [78]. The tea made of boiled roots not only cured venereal disease but also acted as an emetic and physic and served to purify the blood. Among the Kawaiisu, the leaves of the related species *(C. applegatei* ssp. *martinii)* were boiled to make a warm wash to soothe sores [87]. It was also used to make soap [71].

   People in Owens Valley sometimes sucked the base of the stem for its sweetness [65], but anthropologist Julian Steward [66] reported that this species was not used. Some consultants say the colorful and long-lasting flowers of this plant are now used to brighten the home or as a hair decoration [71]. One person said the seeds were eaten, too [71].

Among the Western Shoshone, this plant was known as snake's friend because it grows in the rocks where the rattlesnake lurks. It was thought that the rattlesnake distills its poison from the flower. The flower was used in love charms, and a tea from the flowers made love medicine [58].

Sources: [5] Beatley 1976; [16] Cronquist et al. 1984; [41] Hickman 1993; [42] Jaeger 1941; [53] C. Lynch, pers. commun.; [55] V. Miller, pers. commun.; [58] Murphey 1959; [65] Steward 1933; [66] Steward 1938; [71] Stoffle et al. 1989; [78] Train et al. 1941; [87] Zigmond 1981.

Broomrape Family (Orobanchaceae)

Desert Broomrape
Orobanche cooperi (Gray) Heller

Clustered Broomrape
Orobanche fasciculata Nutt.

Figure 128. Desert broomrape *(Orobanche cooperi)*

Figure 129. The exposed roots of desert broom-rape *(Orobanche cooperi)*

Figures 128, 129

Southern Paiute: *tu'u, du'u* [48, 50]
Western Shoshone: *"doo," "too-ee"* [78]

Description and Habitat

Broomrape (also known as cancer root or Indian asparagus) is a small fleshy herb that is parasitic on the roots of other shrubs [16, 41]. Because broomrape has no chlorophyll, it is not green. It consists of a fleshy stalk or cluster of stalks that are 2–6 inches tall, with stubby purplish nubs that are the rudiments of leaves and clusters of reddish or purple tubular flowers that reveal the plant's close relationship with the figwort family [16, 41]. Broomrape is commonly found in sandy soils beneath or near shrubs in many shrub and woodland communities from 3500 to 8000 feet elevation [5].

Native Uses

The tender stalks of this succulent plant were widely prized for food, with a texture much like asparagus [78]. The whole plant was consumed, especially on hunting trips, because it served as a source of both food and water [9].

Sources: [5] Beatley 1976; [9] Bye 1972; [16] Cronquist et al. 1984; [41] Hickman 1993; [48] Kelly 1964; [50] Laird 1976; [78] Train et al. 1941.

Sunflower Family (Asteraceae)

Mojave Woodyaster

Xylorhiza tortifolia (Torr. & Gray) Greene

Figure 130

Description and Habitat

Mojave woodyaster is a somewhat woody-based perennial herb that grows up to 2 feet high, with white-barked leafy branches [14, 41]. The leaves are elongate and sharply toothed. Asterlike flower heads are borne singly at the top of the long stems. The flower heads are showy, measure up to 2 inches in diameter, and have yellow centers and bluish violet, lavender, or pinkish petals [42]. Mojave woodyaster aster is common in dry rocky areas and washes between 2300 and 4800 feet elevation. It grows with saltbush, creosote bush, wolfberry, spiny hopsage, and blackbrush [5].

Native Uses

Stems of the Mojave woodyaster were crushed to make a topical dressing for cuts or wounds. It is still used for medicinal purposes today [71].

Sources: [5] Beatley 1976; [14] Cronquist 1994; [41] Hickman 1993; [42] Jaeger 1941; [71] Stoffle et al. 1989.

Figure 130. Mojave woodyaster *(Xylorhiza tortifolia)*

HERBACEOUS PLANTS

Sunflower Family (Asteraceae)

New Mexico Thistle
Cirsium neomexicanum Gray

Mojave Thistle
Cirsium mohavense (Greene) Petrak

Figure 131

Owens Valley Paiute: *"coin-yeuh"* [49]
Southern Paiute: *tsiev* [71]; *"chuvia"* [53]; *"chia wugu"* [58]
Timbisha Shoshone: *"zee-ah," "zer-hun"* [49]
Western Shoshone: *"thinna," "tzinga"* [58]

Description and Habitat

Two species of thistle are common in this area. The New Mexico thistle *(Cirsium neomexicanum)* is a biennial with a broad flower head with pale pink to white flowers and a stout stem [14, 41]. It grows in washes, along canyon walls, and sometimes at the edges of rocky ridges in the eastern Mojave

Figure 131. Thistle *(Cirsium neomexicanum)*

Desert and into the southern Great Basin, from 3800 to 6500 feet elevation in most shrub communities [5]. The Mojave thistle *(Cirsium mohavense)* also has a pink to white flower head, but the head is narrower and the stem more slender than that of the New Mexico thistle, and the leaves are armed with sharp yellow spines [14, 41, 42]. It is widely distributed through much of the Mojave Desert [42].

Native Uses

Before the spines hardened, young thistle shoots or stems were peeled and eaten raw [49, 65, 71].

Sources: [5] Beatley 1976; [14] Cronquist 1994; [41] Hickman 1993; [42] Jaeger 1941; [49] Kerr 1936; [53] C. Lynch, pers. commun.; [58] Murphey 1959; [65] Steward 1933; [71] Stoffle et al. 1989.

Poppy Family (Papaveraceae)

Mojave Prickly Poppy
Argemone corymbosa Greene

Flatbud Prickly Poppy
Argemone munita Dur. & Hilg.

Figure 132

Owens Valley Paiute: *"pag-ag-gee"* [49]
Southern Paiute: *kaninimpi* [20]; *"tu-vi-kai-ve"* [53]
Western Shoshone: *"sag-ee-da," "sag-ee-dump," "wya-sag-we-duh,"* *"wya-sag-gee-gee"* [78]

Description and Habitat

True to its name, prickly poppy is a densely stickered herbaceous perennial that grows to about 2–4 feet tall and exudes an orange or yellow sap when broken [41, 42]. The large flowers atop the stem have bright white crinkled petals with a windblown look. The fruits are prickly green capsules full of seeds that are said to be more highly narcotic than opium [42]. Prickly poppy grows in sandy washes and other disturbed habitats. Mojave prickly poppy *(Argemone corymbosa)* is the low-desert form, associated with creosote bush and wolfberry at elevations of 2200–4800 feet. Flatbud prickly poppy *(Argemone munita)* is a higher-desert form, found most commonly in blackbrush or sagebrush scrub or in pinyon-juniper woodlands at 4500–7500 feet elevation [5].

HERBACEOUS PLANTS

Figure 132. Prickly poppy
(Argemone corymbosa)

Native Uses

The Owens Valley Paiute and Kawaiisu terms for prickly poppy mean "rattle," referring to the dried fruit pods full of seeds [65, 87]. Prickly poppy had a wide variety of medicinal uses [78]. The ripe seed was often ground to a paste as a salve for burns, sores, or cuts [49, 87]. Seeds were also roasted, mashed, and eaten as an emetic and physic, or this mixture was made into tiny pills. Two or three of these pills were eaten as a physic. The seeds could be ground and made into a tea used as an eyewash, and a moistened mash of seeds was rubbed into the hair to kill head lice.

Sources: [5] Beatley 1976; [20] DeDecker 1984; [41] Hickman 1993; [42] Jaeger 1941; [49] Kerr 1936; [53] C. Lynch, pers. commun.; [65] Steward 1933; [78] Train et al. 1941; [87] Zigmond 1981.

Spurge Family (Euphorbiaceae)

Whitemargin Sandmat

Chamaesyce albomarginata (Torr. & Gray) Small

Figure 133

Owens Valley Paiute: *"toga-na-tis-oop-ee"* [49]
Southern Paiute: *axghaiv, tuvikaxghaiv* [71]; *"tubicai"* [58];
tava'-namu'obi [47]
Western Shoshone: *"nah-com-boot-zip"* [78]

Description and Habitat

Whitemargin sandmat (also commonly called rattlesnake weed) is a milky
sapped, mat-forming perennial herb 1 inch or less tall but spreading on the
ground to a diameter of 1 foot or more [18, 41]. It bears small round green
leaves on lank alternating branches and develops numerous small white flowers. Whitemargin sandmat is widely distributed and locally common in sandy
soils and washes at low and middle elevations, between 3000 and 6500 feet. It
grows in numerous plant associations dominated by creosote bush, blackbrush, burrobush-wolfberry, saltbush, big sagebrush, and pinyon-juniper
woodlands [5].

Native Uses

Whitemargin sandmat was widely regarded as a remedy for rattlesnake bite;
hence, its alternate common name. The whole plant was crushed and applied

Figure 133. Whitemargin sandmat *(Chamaesyce albomarginata)*

HERBACEOUS PLANTS

to snakebites [77, 86]. The Owens Valley Paiute name for the plant, *"toga-na-tis-oop-ee,"* means "snake medicine" [49]. The plant was also boiled to make a tea used as a tonic [77] or as an eyewash [47, 58]. The leaves, flowers, and milky sap from the stems were used to treat eye inflammations, infections, and cataracts [70]; it is still used today for these purposes.

Sources: [5] Beatley 1976; [18] Cronquist et al. 1997; [41] Hickman 1993; [49] Kerr 1936; [58] Murphey 1959; [70] Stewart 1942; [71] Stoffle et al. 1989; [78] Train et al. 1941; [86] Zigmond 1941.

Flax Family (Linaceae)
Prairie Flax
Linum lewisii Pursh

Figure 134

Owens Valley Paiute: *"poohi natesua"* [55]
Western Shoshone: *"boo-ee nut-ah-zoom,"* *"boo-ee nut-zoo"* [78]

Figure 134. Prairie flax
(Linum lewisii)

Description and Habitat

Prairie flax is a delicate, many-stemmed perennial herb that grows up to 30 inches high [18, 41]. Its leaves are alternate, erect, and narrow, and its five-petaled flowers are white or blue. It is widely distributed, usually as small populations throughout volcanic mountain and mesa areas [5]. Prairie flax is found in washes, near boulders and rock outcrops on flatter terrain, and along cliff bases in canyons from 4500 to 7500 feet elevation. It is associated with sagebrush, pinyon-juniper, and occasionally blackbrush or shadscale communities [5].

Native Uses

Prairie flax is one of the most important plants in the Great Basin for the treatment of sore eyes. The Shoshone name, *"boo-ee nut-ah-zoom,"* can be translated as "eye medicine" [78]. An eyewash was made from the plant by soaking or boiling the stems, leaves, or roots, although a Native consultant at Beatty boiled only the roots to make the wash [78]. Crushed fresh leaves could also be applied to swellings [78]. The stem of prairie flax was steeped to make a tea for curing stomachache and gas [58]. According to Walter Ebeling [22], a fine fiber made of prairie flax (basically linen) was used in twine, rabbit nets, and other string articles.

Sources: [5] Beatley 1976; [18] Cronquist et al. 1997; [22] Ebeling 1986; [41] Hickman 1993; [55] V. Miller, pers. commun.; [58] Murphey 1959; [78] Train et al. 1941.

Goosefoot Family (Chenopodiaceae)

Goosefoot
Chenopodium spp.

Figure 135

Owens Valley Paiute: *ko'yo, waidavi* [65]
Southern Paiute: *"koar," "war"* [9]; *kovi, wara* [48]
Western Shoshone: *üyüp* [66]

Description and Habitat

Goosefoot is an annual herbaceous plant with an erect leafy stem that grows to 8–36 inches high in southern Nevada [41]. Leaves are usually triangular, looking somewhat like a goose's foot. Flowers are small, greenish, and scurfy in appearance and clustered near the top of the stem and branches [41]. The

Figure 135. Goosefoot
(Chenopodium atrovirens)

tiny seeds are black or dark red, circular in outline, and lenticular in cross section, looking like tiny flying saucers.

Several species of goosefoot inhabit different plant communities throughout southern Nevada [5]. Two species, desert goosefoot *(Chenopodium pratericola)* and mealy goosefoot *(Chenopodium incanum)*, grow at lower elevations in Mojave Desert plant communities [5], whereas Fremont's goosefoot *(Chenopodium fremontii)* and pinyon goosefoot *(Chenopodium atrovirens)* grow at higher elevations amid the sagebrush and pygmy woodland communities [5].

Native Uses

Goosefoot was an important food plant for many Native groups in the Great Basin [48, 49]. Both leaves and seeds were eaten. Upper leaves and young plants were often picked in large quantities, boiled, rinsed in cold water, and then fried in grease and salt [87]. Seeds were collected with a seed-beater and basket, then parched and ground to make flour for mush and bread [9]. Goosefoot seeds were broadcast-sown by various Shoshone groups in central

Nevada to increase the yield of this important plant [66]. In Owens Valley, mats made of goosefoot plants were used as shingles to cover the roofs of winter houses [65].

Sources: [5] Beatley 1976; [9] Bye 1972; [41] Hickman 1993; [48] Kelly 1964; [49] Kerr 1936; [65] Steward 1933; [66] Steward 1938; [87] Zigmond 1981.

Nettle Family (Urticaceae)

Stinging Nettle

Urtica dioica L. ssp. *holosericea* (Nutt.) Thorne

Figure 136

Owens Valley Paiute: *"te-na-e-nupe"* [49]
Western Shoshone: *tin'-ai-gop* (stinging hairs) [11]

Description and Habitat

Stinging nettle is an erect semiwoody perennial herb with several stiff square stems that may reach 3–6 feet in height. More or less evenly spaced along each stem are pairs of leaves growing opposite one another, each pair oriented at right angles to the one below. The leaves are lance shaped to ovate, with three to five prominent veins and a crinkly appearance. The small male and female flowers are arrayed in purplish green clusters (catkins) at the leaf nodes. Stinging nettle is found in southern Nevada growing in patches in willow thickets and around streams in the Spring Range and other higher mountains [5].

Both the stems and the undersides of the leaves are covered with bristly hairs, many of which are hollow needles (trichomes) filled with a nasty cocktail of formic acid, various histamines, and other antigenic substances. If one touches or handles the plant, the sharp hairs break off and inject this mix into the skin, resulting in contact dermatitis. The stinging pain, itching, and blistery rash usually lasts for about an hour after contact.

Native Uses

The Kawaiisu counted stinging nettle as one of the four medicines given to people at the Beginning of the World, along with *Datura,* tobacco (*Nicotiana* spp.), and red ants [87]. People slapped fresh nettles on backs, legs, or other areas to relieve soreness (or at least divert attention from it). Poultices of wilted nettles were placed on foreheads to cure headaches and on limbs to ease arthritis [87]. Stinging nettle cured rheumatism on contact [3, 49].

Figure 136. Stinging nettle
(*Urtica dioica* var. *holosericea*)

Fibers obtained from nettle stems make a very strong cord [62], which was used for heavy-duty items such as carrying bags, rabbit nets, and bowstrings [87]. Nearby groups, such as the Cahuilla [4], used the foliage as a tasty and nutritious eating green or tea; when the leaves are cooked or dried, the hairs do not sting.

Sources: [4] Bean and Saubel 1972; [5] Beatley 1976; [11] Chamberlin 1911; [49] Kerr 1936; [62] Palmer 1878; [87] Zigmond 1981.

Buckwheat Family (Polygonaceae)

Willow Dock

Rumex salicifolius Weinm.

Figure 137

Figure 137. Willow dock
(Rumex salicifolius)

Owens Valley Paiute: *atsakan^va* [65]; *"sum-on-ava"* [49]
Southern Paiute: *nambitu* [71]; *kwivavi* [48]
Western Shoshone: *"be-ja-no-ko," "dim-woo-ee,"*
   "enga-pa-wee-ah," "new-wha no-ko" [78]

Description and Habitat

Willow dock (also called Indian rhubarb) is a perennial herb that grows to
2–5 feet high [16, 41]. Its lower leaves are 4–12 inches long and blade
shaped with wavy margins. The native willow dock is found in moist or
wet soils near springs or water. It grows with sagebrush, saltbush, pinyon,
juniper, and occasionally with creosote bush between 3600 and 6800 feet
elevation.

Native Uses

The thick green leaves of willow dock were collected as a potherb and boiled
for greens [49, 71, 87]; they are still collected today for this purpose [71].

The stems were roasted in coals and the inner pulp was eaten hot or cold or the stems were boiled like rhubarb [87]. Seeds were gathered with a seed-beater, parched, and ground in a mortar, then boiled with water to make a thick gravy [87] or baked on stones to make a bread. The leaves can also be eaten raw, cooked into pies or puddings, or dried for later use [43].

The root of water dock was mashed and used as a poultice for a variety of swellings, pains, burns, and bruises. A decoction made of the boiled roots was used for a host of internal problems, especially stomach disorders [65, 78, 87]. A root tea was drunk for rheumatism or used as a tonic [49, 65]. The tea was also used to cure acne in teenagers [55]. Ripe seeds were ground, boiled with water and perhaps some pine resin, and eaten to stop diarrhea [78].

Sources: [16] Cronquist et al. 1984; [41] Hickman 1993; [43] Y. Jake, pers. commun.; [48] Kelly 1964; [49] Kerr 1936; [55] V. Miller, pers. commun.; [65] Steward 1933; [71] Stoffle et al. 1989; [78] Train et al. 1941; [87] Zigmond 1981.

Figwort Family (Scrophulariaceae)
Palmer's Penstemon
Penstemon palmeri Gray

Firecracker Penstemon
Penstemon eatonii Gray

Figures 138, 139

Southern Paiute: *toxo'awatsip, toxopui'bimp* [47]
Western Shoshone: *"toh-quah-bag-um"* [78]

Description and Habitat

Palmer's penstemon (penstemons are also known as beardtongues) is an herbaceous perennial with multiple stems that grow to 2–6 feet tall [16, 41], and its thick triangular leaves are sharply toothed. It bears sweet-scented tubular flowers that are white or pink and often tinged with rose or purple [42]. Each flower has prominent colored lines extending into its throat from its lower lip [41]. Palmer's penstemon grows well in limestone soils and gravelly washes between 3300 and 8000 feet elevation, in creosote bush, sagebrush, pinyon-juniper, and yellow pine–fir communities [5].

Firecracker penstemon is a showy perennial herb having one to several stems arising up to 3 feet high from a basal cluster of leaves [16]. The stem leaves are narrow and untoothed. Each stem bears a string of narrow,

Figure 138. Palmer's pen-
stemon (Penstemon
palmeri)

tubular, brilliant red flowers. Firecracker penstemon is found in sagebrush
steppe, pinyon-juniper woodlands, and pine forests from about 4500 to
8000 feet elevation [5, 16].

Native Uses

Various penstemon species were used as medicine for burns, swelling, sores,
and toothaches [43, 78]. The leaf of Palmer's penstemon was ground up
and put on burns [66]. For fever or snakebite, a pounded poultice was applied externally [47]. Firecracker penstemon and other red-flowered penstemons were boiled and the solution was used to wash burns, easing the pain
and promoting growth of new skin [78]. The Kawaiisu mashed the root of
another scarlet penstemon (Bridge penstemon, *Penstemon rostriflorus*),
mixed it with a little water, and applied it as a poultice to a swollen limb
[87]. Their name for the plant, *pohomatasuk^wi*, means "swelling medicine."

Sources: [5] Beatley 1976; [16] Cronquist et al. 1984; [41] Hickman 1993; [42]
Jaeger 1941; [43] Y. Jake, pers. commun.; [66] Steward 1938; [78] Train et al. 1941;
[87] Zigmond 1981.

HERBACEOUS PLANTS

Figure 139. Firecracker penstemon *(Penstemon eatonii)*

Phlox Family (Polemoniaceae)

Skyrocket Gilia

Ipomopsis aggregata (Pursh) V. Grant

Figure 140

Owens Valley Paiute: *"tsai yarrabuh"* [55]
Southern Paiute: *"shovia navayuna"* [53]; *anka'si'nti* [47]
Western Shoshone: *"enga-moh-wanya," "enga-mutz-o-newie"* [78];
"tem-piute," "tin-ah-piute," "tem-paiute" [58]

Description and Habitat

Skyrocket gilia is a slender erect perennial herb that grows to about 1 foot tall; it has short dissected leaves and numerous 1-inch long, bright red, tubular flowers [16, 41]. The showy flowers, blooming from May to October,

Figure 140. Skyrocket
gilia *(Ipomopsis aggregata)*

have five points resembling a star. Skyrocket gilia grows in dry washes and rocky areas. It is common on the slopes of the northwest Spring Mountains in pinyon-juniper and yellow pine–fir communities between 6000 and 7600 feet elevation [5].

Native Uses

Various parts of this plant were used for medicinal purposes [78]. A tea made from skyrocket gilia, often in combination with green Mormon tea *(Ephedra viridis),* was commonly used as a treatment for venereal disease. The tea was also widely used as an emetic and a physic and for relief of various ailments including stomachache [53, 78]. Skyrocket gilia was also used as a poultice for rheumatic aches and as a purgative. Cold tea of the related ballhead gilia *(Ipomopsis congesta)* was used as an antiseptic wash for cuts, wounds, pimples, and sores and as an eyewash [78].

Sources: [5] Beatley 1976; [16] Cronquist et al. 1984; [41] Hickman 1993; [53] C. Lynch, pers. commun.; [55] V. Miller, pers. commun.; [58] Murphey 1959; [78] Train et al. 1941.

HERBACEOUS PLANTS

Phlox Family (Polemoniaceae)

Longleaf Phlox
Phlox longifolia Nutt.

Figure 141

Owens Valley Paiute: *"paga gibe"* [55]
Western Shoshone: *"din-ah-ee-go," "eye-go-dun-um," "so-go-ron-zee-ah,"*
"so-go-div-oh-sah" [78]

Description and Habitat

Longleaf phlox is a somewhat woody perennial herb that grows to 5–20
inches high [16, 41]. Its linear leaves are about 1 inch long. It often grows
as a compact cushion form (where it sometimes goes by the name Stan-
bury's phlox, *Phlox longifolia* var. *stansburyi* [16]), but is often found
growing up through other shrubs as a taller and more lax plant [41]. Both
forms are conspicuous in the spring and summer mainly by their bright
white to pink flowers. Phlox is widely distributed and common on volcanic
substrates and dry flats and slopes between 4100 and 8000 feet elevation, in
creosote bush, blackbrush, burrobush-wolfberry, sagebrush, and pinyon-
juniper communities [5].

Figure 141. Longleaf
phlox *(Phlox longifolia)*

Native Uses

An eyewash was made by first scraping the roots of longleaf phlox then soaking them in cold water or occasionally by steeping or boiling the scraped roots. A similar decoction was drunk to treat stomachache [78].

Sources: [5] Beatley 1976; [16] Cronquist et al. 1984; [41] Hickman 1993; [55] V. Miller, pers. commun.; [78] Train et al. 1941.

Buttercup Family (Ranunculaceae)

Crimson Columbine
Aquilegia formosa Fischer

Figures 142, 143

Owens Valley Paiute: *"ker-ger-win"* [49]
Southern Paiute: *pawɨhanɨ siŋkadɨ, toha'ama'abɨ* [20]
Western Shoshone: *"enga-moh-wanya," "pah-wah-gum"* [78]

Description and Habitat

Crimson columbine is an herbaceous perennial growing from 8 to 36 inches tall, with pale green lobed leaves in clusters of threes [41, 42]. The showy nodding flowers are composed of five red and yellow petals with back-sweeping spurs and a spray of yellow stamens pointing forward. Columbine is found in moist habitats at the base of cliffs and crevices, around springs and perennial streams, mostly in the pine forests of higher mountains [5].

Native Uses

Columbine served a variety of medicinal uses for Native peoples in the Great Basin. According to Train et al., "The ripe seeds were mashed, moistened, and then rubbed vigorously in the hair to discourage head lice" by people in Death Valley and areas northwest of Yucca Mountain [78]. In other parts of the Great Basin, people used various parts of the plant to stop diarrhea, treat stomachache, cure coughs, ease aching joints, and counteract dizzy spells [78]. The Owens Valley Paiute ate spring shoots as salad greens, according to one source [49].

Sources: [5] Beatley 1976; [20] DeDecker 1984; [41] Hickman 1993; [42] Jaeger 1941; [49] Kerr 1936; [78] Train et al. 1941.

HERBACEOUS PLANTS

Figure 142. Crimson columbine *(Aquilegia formosa)*

Figure 143. Crimson columbine *(Aquilegia formosa)* flower

CHAPTER SEVEN

Grasses and Grasslike Plants

Rush Family (Juncaceae)

Baltic Rush
Juncus balticus Willd.

Figure 144

Owens Valley Paiute: *"sina-va," "whu-kive"* [49];
pawahapu'hia, pawahava, sina'va [65]
Southern Paiute: *pa'sip, parasiev* [71]; *pai'sive* [53]
Western Shoshone: *sonohpi* [71]; *"sineva," "pondaseep"* [58]

Description and Habitat

Baltic rush (also known as wiregrass) is a low, grasslike herb that grows in wet alkaline soils, often as the dominant species [5]. Stems of Baltic rush are round to somewhat flattened, smooth, and dark green and set on coarse

Figure 144. Baltic rush *(Juncus balticus)*

black rhizomes [15]. The leaves are light brown papery sheaths located at the base of the plant. Flowers are small and borne in loose clusters on the side of the upper stem [15]. Baltic rush grows in dense meadows at springs and other wet alkaline places in the southern Great Basin below about 6800 feet elevation [5].

Native Uses

Baltic rush was a common construction material used for baskets, waterfowl decoys, insulation for dwelling walls, and other purposes [71]. The sheath leaves were used to make yellow patterns in basket designs [49] and are still highly valued by some modern basketmakers [71]. Baltic rush was a minor basketmaking material for the Kawaiisu, but little girls often used it while learning to weave [87].

The small seeds of Baltic rush served as food, called *"whu-kive"* [49] or *pawahava* [65] by the Owens Valley Paiute. Stem bases were also apparently eaten [71]. The Owens Valley Paiute made a sweet candy (called *pawahavi-havi* or *sinahavihavi*) from a sugar that forms on the tops of the plants [65].

Sources: [5] Beatley 1976; [15] Cronquist et al. 1977; [49] Kerr 1936; [53] C. Lynch, pers. commun.; [58] Murphey 1959; [65] Steward 1933; [71] Stoffle et al. 1989; [87] Zigmond 1981.

Cattail Family (Typhaceae)
Southern Cattail
Typha domingensis Pers.

Broadleaf Cattail
Typha latifolia L.

Figure 145

Owens Valley Paiute: *toiba* [49]
Southern Paiute: *to?uivɨ* [48]; *to'awve* [53]
Western Shoshone: *toyh* [71]

Description and Habitat

Cattail is a tall perennial aquatic plant that grows in dense colonies up to 10–12 feet tall in standing water or saturated soil [15]. This plant has long straplike leaves and bears its tiny flowers in dense cylindrical spikes up to 1 inch thick and 1 foot long [15]. The upper part of the spike contains the

Figure 145. Broadleaf cattail *(Typha latifolia)*

male pollinating flowers, whereas the lower part contains the female flowers that will eventually become seeds. The brown female spikes ripen in the summer and break open in the fall, releasing millions of tiny seeds along with copious amounts of light brown fluff into the breeze. The southern cattail *(Typha domingensis)* is somewhat taller than the broadleaf cattail *(Typha latifolia)*, with yellowish green leaves less than 0.75 inch wide and golden yellow pollen. It also has flowering spikes with a distinct gap between the male and female flowers [15, 41]. The southern cattail prefers alkaline water or saturated soils at elevations below 3900 feet [5, 15, 41]. The broadleaf cattail has light green flat leaves that are wider than 0.75 inch; it bears spikes having no gap between the male and female flowers and produces orange or yellow pollen [15]. The broadleaf cattail grows in seeps and shallow water from 3900 to 5000 feet elevation [5].

Many parts of the cattail served as food in various seasons. The starchy, tender rhizomes and young shoots were eaten in the winter and spring [49, 65, 71, 87], occasionally also in summer [48]. The pollen, rich in food energy, was collected in summer to make an extremely nutritious cake. The tiny seeds were also eaten. Seeds were collected by flash-burning the fluff, then winnowing in a basket to remove any burned fluff and concentrate the toasted seeds. The Kawaiisu ate green seeds and thought the ripe seeds were no longer good; they also ate the brown flower stalks raw [87]. The Southern Paiute ate the flowering spikes raw [48] or made soup from them [9].

Cattail was also an important raw material for manufacturing. Shoots and stems were used in making decoys, baskets, sweathouse mats, shelters, and boats [55, 71]. Sheaves of cattail leaves were used like shingles to cover houses [65, 87]. Dried stems and fluff were sometimes used as tinder for fire. All parts were dried and stored for use year-round.

Cattails continue to be used and are highly valued today [71]. They figure as sacred plants in modern Sun Dance ceremonies [43].

Sources: [5] Beatley 1976; [9] Bye 1972; [15] Cronquist et al. 1977; [41] Hickman 1993; [43] Y. Jake, pers. commun.; [48] Kelly 1964; [49] Kerr 1936; [53] C. Lynch, pers. commun.; [55] V. Miller, pers. commun.; [65] Steward 1933; [71] Stoffle et al. 1989; [87] Zigmond 1981.

Grass Family (Poaceae)

Inland Saltgrass

Distichlis spicata (L.) Greene

Figure 146

Owens Valley Paiute: *ongavi* [71]
Southern Paiute: *'isuvə* [52]

Description and Habitat

Inland saltgrass is a grayish green sod-forming perennial grass that grows up to about 1 foot tall [15, 41]. Its leaves are narrow, curved, and usually less than 4 inches long. It tolerates seasonally wet alkaline or saline soils, such as those found in salt marshes [15]. Often found growing with fourwing saltbush, inland saltgrass is common at Ash Meadows and other alkaline or wet places in southern Nevada below 6600 feet elevation [5].

Figure 146. Inland saltgrass *(Distichlis spicata)*

Native Uses

The leaves of inland saltgrass yield a salty deposit that was scraped off with sticks while the dew was on the grass. The wet salt was then formed into a ball and cooked in ashes to make a salt supplement [55, 71]. The Kawaiisu used the salt for medicine, not as a seasoning [87]. Grass was pulled out and allowed to dry on a mat. Salt was then beaten off with sticks and winnowed in a basket. The salt was mixed with water and a little sugar, then molded into a cake using a cup or basket hat. Pieces of the salt cake were broken off as desired, then dissolved in water and drunk. This drink acted as a laxative, helped slow the heart, and was enjoyed as a beverage. Children ate pieces of the salt cake like candy. The plant is still used to some extent today [71].

According to one consultant, the Southern Paiute used inland saltgrass to make basketry, matting, rope, sandals, and other utilitarian items [43].

Sources: [5] Beatley 1976; [15] Cronquist et al. 1977; [41] Hickman 1993; [43] Y. Jake, pers. commun.; [52] Lawlor 1995; [55] V. Miller, pers. commun.; [71] Stoffle et al. 1989; [87] Zigmond 1981.

Grass Family (Poaceae)

Common Reed

Phragmites australis (Cav.) Trin. ex Steud.

Figures 147, 148

Owens Valley Paiute: *pihavi* [71]; *hauve* [65];
"*how-o-ba*" [49]; "*pee-havee*" (sugar) [55]
Southern Paiute: *pa'xamp* [71]; "*pa-wy-um-ba*" [53]; "*pahrump*" [58]; *pag-ampi* [48, 50]; "*pah-gump-pea-abbah*," "*pa-gump*,"
"*pa-gump pai-av*" (sugar) [9]
Timbisha Shoshone: "*ha-o-vi*," "*how-oh-vee*" [49]
Western Shoshone: *behabe* [58]

Description and Habitat

Common reed (also known as cane, carrizo grass, or sweet flag) is a tall bamboolike grass that grows to 6–12 feet tall and produces long, purplish white, plumelike blooms [15, 41]. Its leaves are 8–20 inches long and less than 2 inches wide [41]. This perennial grass grows in colonies near wet sites such as seeps and springs in southern Nevada below 4000 feet elevation [5].

Figure 147. Common reed *(Phragmites australis)*

Figure 148. Jack Stewart demonstrates the use of a common reed to start a fire. (Photograph by Julian Steward, courtesy of the University of Illinois Archives)

Native Uses

Common reed has been considered a plant basic to Native American economic life in the Mojave Desert and southern Great Basin [87] and is mentioned in Southern Paiute legend [71]. The canes were indispensable for making arrows [48, 50], fire drills, pipes, and other utilitarian objects [87]. Arrow mainshafts were made of cane, with the thicker end at the forward end of the arrow and a wooden foreshaft inserted into it. Archaeological arrow and dart shafts made of cane are known from Gypsum Cave [36], Pintwater Cave [8], Newberry Cave [19], and elsewhere. In the composite fire drill, a section of cane held a piece of sagebrush (*Artemisia* spp.) wood, which was rotated in a fire hearth to produce heat through rotary friction, thus igniting some tinder. A short section of cane served as the main straight pipe for smoking. Among the Kawaiisu [87], a cane arrow was used to play the musical bow and a split-cane clapper kept the rhythm. At birth, the umbilical cord was cut with a sharpened edge of a split cane. Cane pieces were used as tokens in games of chance and skill. Stems of this large grass were also used to make house walls [71].

GRASSES AND GRASSLIKE PLANTS

Cane was also a major native source of sugar [9, 37, 38, 44, 49, 65, 75, 87]. Anthropologist Julian Steward [65] gave this account:

The sugar, called *hauva-hauva* in Owens Valley, was made from the dried sap brought to the cane surface by small green insects. Green cane was gathered in summer when leaves are thick. The entire plant was cut up and dried until sap lay on the surface in lumps. When ready, the cane was piled on canvas, beaten with sticks to loosen sugar, and then was gathered up, cleaned by winnowing, made into large balls, and stored in shallow baskets, about sixteen inches in diameter, made of tule. (Tule preferred to willow, believing it preserves the sugar but does not give it taste nor change its color.) Now it was ready to eat as candy. The sugar was full of insects, and less sweet than commercial sugar.

Among the Southern Paiute, the sugar was made into a ball about the size of a turkey egg, with "the more aphis in the gob, the better" [75]. The sugar looked like maple sugar and tasted like malted milk [37]. Seeds of cane were also sometimes used for food [43].

Sources: [5] Beatley 1976; [8] Buck and DuBarton 1994; [9] Bye 1972; [15] Cronquist et al. 1977; [19] Davis and Smith 1981; [36] Harrington 1933; [37] Harrington 1945; [38] Heizer 1945; [41] Hickman 1993; [43] Y. Jake, pers. commun.; [44] Jones 1945; [48] Kelly 1964; [49] Kerr 1936; [50] Laird 1976; [53] C. Lynch, pers. commun.; [55] V. Miller, pers. commun.; [58] Murphey 1959; [65] Steward 1933; [71] Stoffle et al. 1989; [75] Stuart 1945; [87] Zigmond 1981.

Grass Family (Poaceae)

Indian Ricegrass
Achnatherum hymenoides (Roemer & J. A. Schultes) Barkworth

Figures 149–151

Owens Valley Paiute: *wai* [65, 71]; "*wye*" [49]
Southern Paiute: *w'ai, wa'iv* [71]; *wai^i* [66]; *wa'a* [50]; *wai'wave* [53]; *wa?aipi* (grass), *wa?ai* (seeds) [48]
Western Shoshone: *wai* [66, 71]

Description and Habitat

Indian ricegrass is a perennial bunchgrass that grows 1–2 feet tall [15]. In spring, it bears a delicate crown of grain on threadlike branchlets above the foliage. The small, hard, dark seeds scatter when this crown is shaken by the wind. This plant prefers dry, sandy soils, tolerates alkaline soils, and is less common on gravelly soils [15]. Ricegrass is one of the most common and

Figure 149. Indian rice-grass *(Achnatherum hymenoides)*

widely distributed perennial grasses in the region [5]. It grows between 2400 and 7500 feet elevation in many vegetation communities [5, 15].

Native Uses

The small seeds of ricegrass were a very important early summer food used by all Native groups in the region [66, 87]. When the seeds were nearly ripe, grass bunches were gathered into a pile, threshed by beating with sticks to loosen the seeds, then winnowed in basket trays to concentrate the seeds. If the seeds were not yet ripe enough, the plants were tied off, cut in bunches, gathered together, and "the grass was scorched, then shaken in the wind to release the seeds" [48, 49, 87]. Seeds were also often gathered by knocking them into a basket with a stick or seed-beater [65, 71] or were taken from caches made by kangaroo rats, located by punching the ground with a digging stick [65].

Ricegrass seeds were pounded lightly to remove the hard outer skin, winnowed in a flat tray, roasted, and ground into flour or stored for later use. The flour was eaten dry or mixed with water or other seeds to make a

Figure 150. Western Shoshone gather bunches of Indian ricegrass into a large pile and thresh it with sticks. (Photograph by Julian Steward, courtesy of the University of Illinois Archives)

Figure 151. Jenny Washburn separates Indian ricegrass seeds from chaff with a broad flat winnowing tray. (Photograph by Julian Steward, courtesy of the University of Illinois Archives)

pudding or gravy. Ricegrass flour also makes delicious "Indian dumplings" [43]. When men in Owens Valley went "on hunting trips a ground up mixture of *wye,* taboose [grass-nuts, or *Cyperus esculentus*], and sagebrush seeds (dry) was carried and mixed with water when ready for use" [49]. Stands of ricegrass were managed by sowing seeds and burning areas to stimulate growth [66, 71]. According to Stoffle et al., the seeds are still harvested by some Native Great Basin people [71].

Sources: [5] Beatley 1976; [15] Cronquist et al. 1977; [43] Y. Jake, pers. commun.; [48] Kelly 1964; [49] Kerr 1936; [50] Laird 1976; [53] C. Lynch, pers. commun.; [65] Steward 1933; [66] Steward 1938; [71] Stoffle et al. 1989; [87] Zigmond 1981.

Grass Family (Poaceae)

Desert Needlegrass

Achnatherum speciosum (Trin. & Rupr.) Barkworth

Figure 152

Owens Valley Paiute: *huki* [65]
Southern Paiute: *monomp* [71]; *monompɨ* [50]; *howuve* [53]

Description and Habitat

This leafy perennial bunchgrass typically grows to about 2 feet tall, with narrow spikes of grain rising above the foliage [15]. Long bent bristles, or awns, are attached to the long pointed seeds. Desert needlegrass is a common and widely distributed desert grass of middle elevations, particularly on dry slopes. It grows between 3500 and 6000 feet elevation with blackbrush and less commonly with spiny hopsage, wolfberry, and sagebrush [5].

Native Uses

Seeds of desert needlegrass were an important food plant for the Owens Valley Paiute, who favored it for mush [65]. The seeds were harvested for food in late spring. Bunches of grass were cut, tied together, and carried in a large burden basket. They were spread out on flat rocks to dry, then threshed by burning. Burned stalks were stirred and lifted to let the seeds fall out. Seeds were then gathered and winnowed. When boiled, the seeds swelled like rice. Sometimes, seeds were ground to a meal before cooking. One Southern Paiute consultant [43] thought the seeds were used to make a thin mush or gravy, but others denied the use of needlegrass for food except by horses [52, 53].

Figure 152. Desert needlegrass *(Achnatherum speciosum)*

The grass was also used by the Owens Valley Paiute to line storage pits for pine nuts; hence, the name *huki'va* for these pits [65]. Southern Paiute people used the roots to make hairbrushes [71].

Sources: [5] Beatley 1976; [15] Cronquist et al. 1977; [43] Y. Jake, pers. commun.; [50] Laird 1976; [52] Lawlor 1995; [53] C. Lynch, pers. commun.; [65] Steward 1933; [71] Stoffle et al. 1989.

Grass Family (Poaceae)

Basin Wild Rye
Leymus cinereus (Scribn. & Merr.) A. Löve

Figure 153

Owens Valley Paiute: *waiya* [65, 66]
Southern Paiute: *wavi* [48]; *wa'hive* [53]
Western Shoshone: *wa:vi* [66]

Description and Habitat

Basin wild rye is a tall grass that grows in large clumps, 3–6 feet high and as much as 3 feet in diameter [15, 41]. This conspicuous perennial grass prefers volcanic substrates along streams, canyons, roadsides, sagebrush shrubland, and open woodlands below 9000 feet elevation [5]. It also grows in

Figure 153. Basin
wild rye *(Leymus
cinereus)*

alkaline and saline soils and can be found growing in small populations
along washes, in depressions, or near springs [5].

Native Uses

Seeds of wild rye served as a valued food source throughout the Great Basin
[65], but less so in the Mojave Desert to the south [87]. Bundles of wild rye
were made into shingles to cover houses in both winter and summer in
Owens Valley and elsewhere [65]. Sheaves of grass also served as bedding or
matting [43], especially in the northern Great Basin [66]. The sturdy stems
were used in making cradleboards [43].

Sources: [5] Beatley 1976; [15] Cronquist et al. 1977; [41] Hickman 1993;
[43] Y. Jake, pers. commun.; [48] Kelly 1964; [53] C. Lynch, pers. commun.;
[65] Steward 1933; [66] Steward 1938; [87] Zigmond 1981.

CHAPTER EIGHT

Bulb Plants

Lily Family (Liliaceae)

Winding Mariposa Lily
Calochortus flexuosus S. Wats.

Figure 154

Owens Valley Paiute: *kogi* [58, 71]; *"ko-gio"* [56]; *"akaa-huna-diew"*
    (for *Calochortus kennedyi*) [49]
Southern Paiute: *sixo'o* [71]; *"se-go-a"* [53]; *sigoʔo* [48]
Timbisha Shoshone: *"koh-gee," "ko-kee"* (for *Calochortus kennedyi*) [49]; *kogwi*
    (for *Calochortus kennedyi*) [66]; *"sea-go"* (for *Calochortus nuttallii*) [49]
Western Shoshone: *sigo* [71]

Description and Habitat

The winding mariposa blooms in the spring from a deeply set bulb, sending
up two or three narrow leaves and a long stem that meanders along the
ground or twines through bushes [15, 42]. This lily is topped by a stun-
ningly beautiful cup-shaped blossom of white to delicate purple hue [15].
Several other species of mariposa lily grow in the southern Great Basin and
Mojave Desert, with spring blooms of scarlet, yellow, or ivory [42]. The
winding mariposa is common between 3300 and 6500 feet elevation in desert shrub communities associated with blackbrush and sagebrush [15, 41]. It
is less commonly found in warm-desert shrub environments such as the creosote bush–wolfberry–spiny hopsage or wolfberry– spiny hopsage associations [5]. The winding mariposa often prefers rocky soils, but is also common in well-drained alluvial soils in valleys.

Native Uses

Mariposa lily bulbs were widely used as food, and to some extent, they are
still collected today [71]. The seeds of the desert mariposa lily *(Calochortus
kennedyi)* were also eaten, according to one report [49]. Bulbs were eaten
raw or cooked by boiling, roasting in ashes, or sometimes steaming in a special earthen oven [48]. The bulbs were also boiled and the liquid drunk as a

Figure 154. Winding mariposa lily *(Calochortus flexuosus)*

thin soup when traveling in the mountains [43]. The species used most often include the desert mariposa lily and sego lily *(Calochortus nuttallii)*, but winding mariposa bulbs were also eaten by Native people [42]. The bulb of this plant is deeply set in the ground and is often offset from the stem of the plant by a lateral rhizome, making it difficult to find when digging in the rocky and calichified ground typical of the Mojave Desert. But where the bulbs are more abundant or in loose sandy soil, "they grow in beds, and one can do blind digging on them after locating even one seed stalk" [58].

Sources: [5] Beatley 1976; [15] Cronquist et al. 1977; [41] Hickman 1993; [42] Jaeger 1941; [43] Y. Jake, pers. commun.; [48] Kelly 1964; [49] Kerr 1936; [53] C. Lynch, pers. commun.; [56] B. Moose, pers. commun.; [58] Murphey 1959; [66] Steward 1938; [71] Stoffle et al. 1989.

Lily Family (Liliaceae)
Nevada Onion
Allium nevadense S. Wats.

Figure 155

Owens Valley Paiute: *paiduci* [65]; *"paileese," "paidise"* [49]
Southern Paiute: *kwičasɨ, kwičas* [48]; *"nin-youg"* [53]
Western Shoshone: *gunk:* [66]

Figure 155. Nevada onion
(Allium nevadense)

Description and Habitat

Like all wild onions, the Nevada onion is a perennial plant that overwinters as a small layered bulb and sprouts in the spring. It sends up a single leaf that is somewhat rounded in cross section, often with a coiled tip [15]. It produces a flowering stem that bears a terminal cluster of whitish to pinkish flowers with a deep pink midrib [15]. The Nevada onion prefers sandy or rocky soils, especially near washes, between 4000 to 7000 feet elevation, in blackbrush or sagebrush scrub or pinyon-juniper woodlands [5]. It is occasionally found associated with creosote bush or saltbush at lower elevations [5]. Other species of wild onion may grow in the region in small localized populations [5].

Native Uses

The bulbs and greens of several different wild onion species, including the Nevada onion, were a favored spring food of Native Great Basin groups, although not a staple crop [49, 65, 66, 87]. Bulbs were gathered using a digging stick [65]. Some Native consultants in the western Mojave Desert and

Owens Valley indicated that the greens, not the bulbs, were sought [56, 87]. Either way, greens and bulbs were both eaten fresh. Among some Southern Paiute groups, the roots were sometimes boiled or roasted in an earthen oven [48]. Native people still commonly use wild onions in salads and other dishes today [43].

Sources: [5] Beatley 1976; [15] Cronquist et al. 1977; [43] Y. Jake, pers. commun.; [48] Kelly 1964; [49] Kerr 1936; [53] C. Lynch, pers. commun.; [56] B. Moose, pers. commun.; [65] Steward 1933; [66] Steward 1938; [87] Zigmond 1981.

Lily Family (Liliaceae)

Desert Hyacinth

Dichelostemma pulchellum (Salisb.) Heller

Figure 156

Owens Valley Paiute: *tupusi, sigo* [65, 66]
Timbisha Shoshone: *"see-go," "see-va-pea"* [49]
Western Shoshone: *sigo* [66, 71]

Description and Habitat

Desert hyacinth (also commonly known as bluedicks) is a liliaceous plant found in many shrubby plant communities in the southern Great Basin [42]. It grows in the spring from small pea- to marble-sized bulbs (or corms). Desert hyacinth is recognized by two or three narrow slightly keeled leaves and a leafless stalk, 1–2 feet tall, that bears a cluster of small blue flowers at the top [15, 41]. Desert hyacinth tends to grow in small but dense local populations in shrubby plant communities between 3500 and 6800 feet elevation [5]. It is commonly found growing among rocks on volcanic ridgetops or on well-drained alluvial substrates, in spiny hopsage–wolfberry, creosote bush–spiny hopsage–wolfberry, and blackbrush plant associations [5].

Native Uses

People dug up the corms of desert hyacinth in the spring or fall with long wooden digging sticks, or they robbed caches of corms collected by rats or gophers [66]. This plant was a very important food source in Owens Valley, where extensive stands were carefully irrigated and tended [65]. Because the corms are storable for long periods, they were sometimes eaten raw when fresh, but the greater part of the harvest was stored and dried for later use. Dried desert hyacinth corms are nutritious and tasty, with a nutlike flavor.

According to one source [49], however, the underground stalk was cooked, but not the hard bulbs, which were seldom eaten for fear of damaging the teeth. (Dried bulbs can be extremely hard.) It is likely that dried bulbs were not eaten whole, but were instead ground into flour [66].

The starchy corms of desert hyacinth were also rubbed on a metate to make glue, which was spread on seed-gathering baskets to fill holes. After hardening, the glue created a translucent film [87].

Sources: [5] Beatley 1976; [15] Cronquist et al. 1977; [41] Hickman 1993; [42] Jaeger 1941; [49] Kerr 1936; [65] Steward 1933; [66] Steward 1938; [71] Stoffle et al. 1989; [87] Zigmond 1981.

References

1. Barneby, Rupert. 1989. Fabales. In *Intermountain Flora: Vascular Plants of the Intermountain West, U.S.A., vol. 3, part B,* by Arthur Cronquist, Arthur A. Holmgren, Noel H. Holmgren, James L. Reveal, and Patricia K. Holmgren. Bronx, N.Y.: The New York Botanical Garden.
2. Barrows, David P. 1967. *The Ethno-Botany of the Coahuilla Indians of Southern California.* 1900. Reprint, Banning, Calif.: Malki Museum Press.
3. Bean, Lowell John, and Katherine Siva Saubel. 1963. Cahuilla Ethnobotanical Notes: Aboriginal Use of Mesquite and Screwbean. *University of California Archaeological Survey Annual Report* 1962–1963: 51–78.
4. Bean, Lowell John, and Katherine Siva Saubel. 1972. *Temelpakh: Cahuilla Indian Knowledge and Usage of Plants.* Banning, Calif.: Malki Museum Press.
5. Beatley, Janice C. 1976. *Vascular Plants of the Nevada Test Site and Central-Southern Nevada: Ecologic and Geographic Distributions.* TID-26881, U.S. Energy Research and Development Administration, Division of Biomedical and Environmental Research. Springfield, Va.: National Technical Information Service, U.S. Department of Commerce.
6. Bell, Willis H., and Edward F. Castetter. 1937. The Utilization of Mesquite and Screwbean by the Aborigines in the American Southwest: Ethnobiological Studies in the American Southwest. V. *University of New Mexico Bulletin, Biological Series* 4(5): 3–63.
7. Benson, Lyman, and Robert A. Darrow. 1981. *Trees and Shrubs of the Southwestern Deserts.* 3rd ed. Tucson: University of Arizona Press.
8. Buck, Paul E., and Anne DuBarton. 1994. Archaeological Investigations at Pintwater Cave, Nevada, During the 1963–64 Field Season. *Journal of California and Great Basin Anthropology* 16(2): 221–42.
9. Bye, Robert A., Jr. 1972. Ethnobotany of the Southern Paiute Indians in the 1870s, with a Note on the Early Ethnobotanical Contributions of Dr. Edward Palmer. In *Great Basin Cultural Ecology: A Symposium,* edited by Don D. Fowler, 87–104. Desert Research Institute Publications in the Social Sciences no. 8. Reno, Nev.: Desert Research Institute.
10. Castetter, Edward F., and Willis H. Bell. 1951. *Yuman Indian Agriculture: Primitive Subsistence on the Lower Colorado and Gila Rivers.* Albuquerque: University of New Mexico Press.
11. Chamberlin, Ralph V. 1911. The Ethno-botany of the Gosiute Indians. *Proceedings of the Philadelphia Academy of Natural Science* 63: 24–99.
12. Coville, Frederick V. 1892. The Panamint Indians of California. *American Anthropologist* 5: 351–61.

13. Coville, Frederick V. 1893. *Botany of the Death Valley Expedition.* Contributions of the U.S. National Herbarium no. 4. Washington, D.C.: U.S. Department of Agriculture.

14. Cronquist, Arthur. 1994. Asterales. In *Intermountain Flora: Vascular Plants of the Intermountain West, U.S.A., vol. 5,* by Arthur Cronquist, Arthur A. Holmgren, Noel H. Holmgren, James L. Reveal, and Patricia K. Holmgren. Bronx, N.Y.: The New York Botanical Garden.

15. Cronquist, Arthur, Arthur A. Holmgren, Noel H. Holmgren, James L. Reveal, and Patricia K. Holmgren. 1977. *Intermountain Flora: Vascular Plants of the Intermountain West, U.S.A., vol. 6, The Monocotyledons.* Bronx, N.Y.: The New York Botanical Garden.

16. Cronquist, Arthur, Arthur A. Holmgren, Noel H. Holmgren, James L. Reveal, and Patricia K. Holmgren. 1984. *Intermountain Flora: Vascular Plants of the Intermountain West, U.S.A., vol. 4, Subclass Asteridae (Except Asterales).* Bronx, N.Y.: The New York Botanical Garden.

17. Cronquist, Arthur, Arthur A. Holmgren, Noel H. Holmgren, and James L. Reveal. 1986. *Intermountain Flora: Vascular Plants of the Intermountain West, U.S.A., vol. 1.* Bronx, N.Y.: The New York Botanical Garden.

18. Cronquist, Arthur, Noel H. Holmgren, and Patricia K. Holmgren. 1997. *Intermountain Flora: Vascular Plants of the Intermountain West, U.S.A., vol. 3, part A, Subclass Rosidae (except Fabales).* Bronx, N.Y.: The New York Botanical Garden.

19. Davis, C. Alan, and Gerald A. Smith. 1981. *Newberry Cave.* Redlands, Calif.: San Bernardino County Museum Association.

20. DeDecker, Mary. 1984. *Flora of the Northern Mojave Desert, California.* Special Publication no. 7. Berkeley: California Native Plant Society.

21. Dutcher, B. H. 1893. Piñon Gathering among the Panamint. *American Anthropologist* 6: 377–80.

22. Ebeling, Walter. 1986. *Handbook of Indian Foods and Fibers of Arid America.* Berkeley: University of California Press.

23. El-Ghomeini, A. A., A. Wallace, and E. M. Romney. 1980. Multivariate Analysis of the Vegetation in a Two-Desert Interface. *Great Basin Naturalist Memoirs* 4: 42–58.

24. El-Ghomeini, A. A., A. Wallace, and E. M. Romney. 1980. Socio-ecological and Soil-Plant Studies of the Natural Vegetation in the Northern Mojave Desert–Great Basin Desert Interface. *Great Basin Naturalist Memoirs* 4: 73–87.

25. Esteves, Pauline. 1998. Personal communication.

26. Farris, Glenn J. 1980. A Reassessment of the Nutritional Value of *Pinus monophylla. Journal of California and Great Basin Anthropology* 2(1): 132–37.

27. Felger, Richard Stephen. 1977. Mesquite in Indian Cultures of Southwestern North America. In *Mesquite: Its Biology in Two Desert Scrub Ecosystems,* edited by B. B. Simpson, 150–76. Stroudsburg, Pa.: Dowden, Hutchinson, and Ross.

28. Felger, Richard Stephen, and Mary Beck Moser. 1985. *People of the Desert and Sea: Ethnobotany of the Seri Indians.* Tucson: University of Arizona Press.

29. Fowler, Catherine S. 1972. *Comparative Numic Ethnobiology.* Ph.D. diss., University of Pittsburgh, Pittsburgh, Pa.

30. Fowler, Catherine S. 1972. Some Ecological Clues to Proto-Numic homelands. In *Great Basin Cultural Ecology: A Symposium,* edited by Don D.

Fowler, 105–22. Desert Research Institute Publications in the Social Sciences no. 8. Reno, Nev.: Desert Research Institute.

31. Fowler, Catherine S. 1986. Subsistence. In *Handbook of North American Indians, vol. 11, Great Basin,* edited by Warren d'Azevedo, 64–97. Washington, D.C.: Smithsonian Institution Press.

32. Fowler, Catherine S. 1995. Some Notes on Ethnographic Subsistence Systems in Mojavean Environments in the Great Basin. *Journal of Ethnobiology* 15(1): 99–117.

33. Fowler, Catherine S. 1996. Historical Perspectives on Timbisha Shoshone Land Management Practices, Death Valley, California. In *Case Studies in Environmental Archaeology,* edited by Elizabeth J. Reitz, Lee A. Newsom, and Sylvia Scudder, 87–101. New York: Plenum.

34. Fowler, Don D., and Catherine S. Fowler, eds. 1971. *Anthropology of the Numa: John Wesley Powell's Manuscripts on the Numic Peoples of Western North America, 1868–1880.* Smithsonian Contributions to Anthropology no. 14. Washington, D.C.: Smithsonian Institution.

35. Fox, A., C. Heron, and M. Q. Sutton. 1995. Characterization of Natural Products on Native American Archaeological and Ethnographic Materials from the Great Basin, U.S.A.: A Preliminary Study. *Archaeometry* 37(2): 363–75.

36. Harrington, Mark Raymond. 1933. *Gypsum Cave, Nevada.* Southwest Museum Papers no. 8. Los Angeles, Calif.: Southwest Museum.

37. Harrington, Mark Raymond. 1945. Bug Sugar. *The Masterkey* 19: 95–96.

38. Heizer, Robert F. 1945. Honey-Dew Sugar in Western North America. *The Masterkey* 19: 141–45.

39. Hessing, Mark B., and Greg T. Sharp. 1997. *Classification and Map of Vegetation at Yucca Mountain, Nevada.* Report prepared for the U.S. Department of Energy, Yucca Mountain Site Characterization Project, by TRW Environmental Safety Systems, Inc., Las Vegas, Nev.

40. Hessing, Mark B., Glen E. Lyon, Greg T. Sharp, W. Kent Ostler, Ronald A. Green, and Jay P. Angerer. 1996. *The Vegetation of Yucca Mountain: Description and Ecology.* Report prepared for the U.S. Department of Energy, Yucca Mountain Site Characterization Project, by TRW Environmental Safety Systems, Inc., Las Vegas, Nev.

41. Hickman, James C. 1993. *The Jepson Manual: Higher Plants of California.* Berkeley: University of California Press.

42. Jaeger, Edmund C. 1941. *Desert Wild Flowers.* Rev. ed. Palo Alto, Calif.: Stanford University Press.

43. Jake, Yetta. 1998. Personal communication.

44. Jones, Volney A. 1945. The Use of Honey-Dew as Food by Indians. *The Masterkey* 19: 145–49.

45. Jones, Volney A. 1948. Notes of Frederick S. Dellenbaugh on the Southern Paiute from Letters of 1927 and 1928. *The Masterkey* 22: 177–82.

46. Kelly, Isabel T. 1932–1934. Unpublished field notes. University of California, Berkeley, Archives Microfilm CU 23.1 no. 138.

47. Kelly, Isabel T. 1939. Southern Paiute Shamanism. *University of California Anthropological Records* 2(4): 151–67.

48. Kelly, Isabel T. 1964. *Southern Paiute Ethnography.* University of Utah Anthropological Papers no. 69. Salt Lake City: University of Utah.

49. Kerr, Mark. ca. 1936. Unpublished notes. Eastern California Museum, Independence, Calif.
50. Laird, Carobeth. 1976. *The Chemehuevis.* Banning, Calif.: Malki Museum Press.
51. Laird, Carobeth. 1984. *Mirror and Pattern: George Laird's World of Chemehuevi Mythology.* Banning, Calif.: Malki Museum Press.
52. Lawlor, Elizabeth J. 1995. *Archaeological Site-Formation Processes Affecting Plant Remains in the Mojave Desert.* Ph.D. diss., University of California, Riverside.
53. Lynch, Cynthia. 1998. Personal communication.
54. Madsen, David B. 1986. Great Basin Nuts: A Short Treatise on the Distribution, Productivity, and Prehistoric Use of Pinyon. In *Anthropology of the Desert West: Essays in Honor of Jesse D. Jennings,* edited by Carol J. Condie and Don D. Fowler, 21–42. Salt Lake City: University of Utah Press.
55. Miller, Vernon. 1998. Personal communication.
56. Moose, Bertha. 1998. Personal communication.
57. Mozingo, Hugh N. 1987. *Shrubs of the Great Basin: A Natural History.* Reno: University of Nevada Press.
58. Murphey, Edith Van Allen. 1959. *Indian Uses of Native Plants.* Palm Desert, Calif.: Desert Printers, Inc.
59. Musser-Lopez, R. A. 1983. Yaaʔvya's Poro: The Singular Power Object of a Chemehuevi Shaman. *Journal of California and Great Basin Anthropology* 5: 260–64.
60. O'Donnell, John Thomas, Mark Q. Sutton, and R. W. Robinson. 1997. Eggshell Cave: A Ceremonial Site in the Western Mojave Desert, California. *Journal of California and Great Basin Anthropology* 19(1): 104–16.
61. Palmer, Edward. 1871. Food Products of the North American Indians. In *Report of the Commissioner of Agriculture for 1870,* 404–28. Washington, D.C.: U.S. Department of Agriculture.
62. Palmer, Edward. 1878. Plants Used by the Indians of the United States. *American Naturalist* 12: 593–606, 646–55.
63. Shearin, Nancy L. 1990. A Crookneck Wooden Staff from San Juan County, Utah. *Utah Archaeology* 3(1): 111–22.
64. Simms, Steven R. 1987. *Behavioral Ecology and Hunter-Gatherer Foraging: An Example from the Great Basin.* British Archaeological Reports, International Series no. 381. Oxford, U.K.: British Archaeological Reports.
65. Steward, Julian H. 1933. Ethnography of the Owens Valley Paiute. *University of California Publications in American Archaeology and Ethnology* 33: 233–350.
66. Steward, Julian H. 1938. *Basin-Plateau Aboriginal Sociopolitical Groups.* Bureau of American Ethnology Bulletin no. 120. Washington, D.C.: Smithsonian Institution.
67. Steward, Julian H. 1941. Culture Element Distributions. XIII. Nevada Shoshoni. *University of California Anthropological Records* 4(2): 209–59.
68. Stewart, Kenneth M. 1965. Mohave Indian Gathering of Wild Plants. *The Kiva* 31: 46–53.
69. Stewart, Kenneth M. 1983. Mohave. In *Handbook of North American Indians, vol. 10, Southwest,* edited by Alfonso Ortiz, 55–70. Washington, D.C.: Smithsonian Institution Press.

70. Stewart, Omer C. 1942. Culture Element Distributions. XVIII. Ute–Southern Paiute. *University of California Anthropological Records* 6(4): 231–360.
71. Stoffle, Richard W., Michael J. Evans, David B. Halmo, Wesley E. Niles, and Joan T. O'Farrell. 1989. *Native American Plant Resources in the Yucca Mountain Area, Nevada*. Report DOE/NV-10576-19. Las Vegas, Nev.: U.S. Department of Energy, Nevada Operations Office.
72. Stoffle, Richard W., David B. Halmo, Michael J. Evans, and John E. Olmsted. 1990. Calculating the Cultural Significance of American Indian Plants: Paiute and Shoshone Ethnobotany at Yucca Mountain, Nevada. *American Anthropologist* 92: 418–32.
73. Stuart, Bradley R. 1945. Pug-A-Roo Picks Mescal. *The Masterkey* 19: 79–81.
74. Stuart, Bradley R. 1945. Pug-A-Roo Picks Pine-Nuts. *The Masterkey* 19: 155.
75. Stuart, Bradley R. 1945. Southern Paiute Staff of Life. *The Masterkey* 19: 133–34.
76. Sutton, Mark Q. 1990. Notes on Creosote Lac Scale Insect Resin as a Mastic and Sealant in the Southwestern Great Basin. *Journal of California and Great Basin Anthropology* 12(2): 262–68.
77. Tilford, Gregory L. 1997. *Edible and Medicinal Plants of the West*. Missoula, Mont.: Mountain Press.
78. Train, Percy, James H. Henrichs, and W. Andrew Archer. 1941. *Medicinal Uses of Plants by Indian Tribes of Nevada*. Contributions toward a Flora of Nevada no. 33. Washington, D.C.: Division of Plant Exploration and Introduction, Bureau of Plant Industry, U.S. Department of Agriculture.
79. Van Valkenburgh, Richard F. 1976. Chemehuevi Notes. In *Paiute Indians, vol. II*, edited by David Agee Horr, 225–53. American Indian Ethnohistory Series: California and Basin-Plateau Indians. New York: Garland.
80. Vasek, Frank C. 1980. Creosote Bush: Long-Lived Clones in the Mojave Desert. *American Journal of Botany* 28: 133–48.
81. Wallace, William J. 1953. Tobacco and Its Use among the Mohave Indians. *The Masterkey* 27: 193–202.
82. Welsh, Stanley L., N. Duane Atwood, Sherel Goodrich, and Larry C. Higgins, eds. 1987. *A Utah Flora*. Great Basin Naturalist Memoir no. 9. Provo, Utah: Brigham Young University.
83. Wheat, Margaret M. 1967. *Survival Arts of the Primitive Paiutes*. Reno: University of Nevada Press.
84. Wilke, Philip. 1988. Bow Staves Harvested from Juniper Trees by Indians of Nevada. *Journal of California and Great Basin Anthropology* 10: 3–31.
85. Yohe, Robert M., II 1997. Archaeological Evidence of Aboriginal Cultigen Use in Late Nineteenth and Early Twentieth Century Death Valley, California. *Journal of Ethnobiology* 17: 267–82.
86. Zigmond, Maurice L. 1941. *Ethnobotanical Studies among California and Great Basin Shoshoneans*. Ph.D. diss., Yale University, New Haven, Conn.
87. Zigmond, Maurice L. 1981. *Kawaiisu Ethnobotany*. Salt Lake City: University of Utah Press.